BRAVING THE NEW WORLD

BRAVING THE NEW WORLD

1619-1784

FROM THE ARRIVAL OF THE ENSLAVED AFRICANS
TO THE END OF THE AMERICAN REVOLUTION

Don Nardo

CHELSEA HOUSE PUBLISHERS
New York   Philadelphia

FRONTISPIECE Allowed a rare breath of fresh air, Africans continue the "middle passage"—the sea journey from Africa to America. Some individuals reacted to the nightmarish voyage by simply staring into space, a condition known to their captors as "fixed melancholy."

ON THE COVER The first captured Africans to reach North America arrive in Virginia in 1619. In the beginning, white settlers treated blacks as indentured servants, but the relationship soon evolved into a system of slavery based on race.

Chelsea House Publishers
Editorial Director Richard Rennert
Executive Managing Editor Karyn Gullen Browne
Copy Chief Robin James
Picture Editor Adrian G. Allen
Art Director Robert Mitchell
Manufacturing Director Gerald Levine

Milestones in Black American History
Senior Editor Marian W. Taylor
Series Originator and Adviser Benjamin I. Cohen
Series Consultants Clayborne Carson, Darlene Clark Hine
Series Designer Rae Grant

Staff for BRAVING THE NEW WORLD
Editorial Assistant Annie McDonnell
Picture Researcher Villette Harris

First Printing

1 3 5 7 9 8 6 4 2

Library of Congress Cataloging-in-Publication Data

Nardo, Don, 1947–
    Braving the New World, 1619–1784: from the arrival of the enslaved Africans to the end of the American Revolution/Don Nardo.
        p. cm.—(Milestones in Black American history)
    Includes bibliographical references and index.
    ISBN 0-7910-2259-5.
        ISBN 0-7910-2685-X (pbk.)
    1. Slavery—United States—History—Juvenile literature. 2. Afro-Americans—History—To 1863—Juvenile literature. [1. Slavery. 2. Afro-Americans—History—To 1863.] I. Title. II. Series.
E446.N35 1994
973'.0496073—dc20   94-2963
                                                                      CIP
                                                                      AC

CONTENTS

MILESTONES IN BLACK AMERICAN HISTORY

INTRODUCTION

America's colonial period starts with the establishment of the first English settlements in the New World. Over the next century and a half, Americans developed their own social traditions, economic practices, and laws; on these, they built a foundation for the powerful nation that would emerge from the revolution that started in 1775. The colonists' legacy included a spirit of independence, courage, endurance, ingenuity, and boundless enthusiasm for what lay ahead. But along with these keys to a golden future, the legacy carried the seeds of evil.

Introduced to North America in 1619, black slavery would darken the fabric of American life like a spreading bloodstain. The nation had been founded by people who loved liberty, but it became a place where human beings could be bought and sold.

The African slave trade began not with the English colonists but centuries earlier, when Arabs and various African and European peoples forced blacks into servitude. Eventually, European sugar planters in the Caribbean and South America began to import large numbers of black slaves, men and women who were deprived of their human rights, forced to live in deplorable conditions, and made to work until they dropped.

For their labor needs, early North American colonists relied on indentured servants—poor whites who traded years of labor for a passage to America—and black slavery grew slowly. At first, blacks and whites worked side by side, and people of both races often earned their freedom and set up farms or trades of their own. Some blacks even acquired their own slaves. Then, in the late 1600s, white immigration dropped sharply, and planters began to acquire black slaves; by 1710, the southern colonies had developed thriving plantation economies, largely supported by slave labor. At the same time, the northern colonies were moving from agriculture to industry and commerce and steadily reducing their interest in slaves.

As the southern slave population expanded, whites began to see blacks as a potential threat. Slaves who broke the rules—resisting, running away, or attacking a white person—could be whipped, maimed, branded, or even executed. But despite indignities and cruel treatment, most slaves made the best of their situation. Developing their own work routines, many learned such occupations as weaving, baking, blacksmithing, ship building, and printing. Eventually, slaves contributed so much to the southern economy that the region depended on them completely.

America's blacks came from a number of African regions, but in the New World they developed a sense of community and produced a culture all their own. Most blacks continued to practice African religions, although by the end of the colonial period many had converted to Christianity.

In 1770, five years before the outbreak of the American Revolution, a free northern black man, Crispus Attucks, led a crowd of resentful Bostonians in taunting a group of British soldiers. In what became known as the Boston Massacre, the angry redcoats opened fire, killing Attucks and four others and making Attucks the first martyr for American freedom. When the Revolution began, blacks all over the country volunteered to fight for independence; eventually, some 5,000 African Americans served, many with great distinction.

At this point, northerners were questioning the morality of the "peculiar institution," and a large number freed their slaves. Southern plantation owners, however, continued to be dependent on their black workers. With the close of the war in 1783, the United States was born, but it was a nation divided from the start. A crucial key to its future was its population—then predominantly in chains—of millions of African Americans.

MILESTONES
1619-1784

1619 • The first slave ship to land on the American mainland brings 20 captive Africans to Jamestown. At first, blacks make up only a small part of the colony's workforce, as most labor is still performed by white indentured servants paying off their passage to the New World.

1625 • Virginia's census lists only 23 blacks, reflecting tobacco planters' continued reliance on indentured servants rather than on imported Africans.

1627 • The English situate their first sugar colony on Barbados; Jamaica, St. Croix, Guadeloupe, and other Caribbean islands are soon claimed by European nations eager to profit from the sugar industry. Of the approximately 12 million enslaved Africans brought to the New World between 1450 and 1870, fully half go to these "sugar islands."

1662 • Virginia passes a law denying "mulattoes," people of mixed races, the chance to gain freedom on the ground that their fathers were white.

1664 • Maryland passes a law requiring all slaves to serve for life. Because fewer masters subsequently free their slaves, the number of free blacks begins to decline.

1666 • London's Great Fire of 1666 creates many jobs in England, where workers are needed to rebuild the city. More job opportunities, as well as higher wages and lower British birth rates, cause fewer whites to emigrate as indentured servants, which, in turn, increases the need for slave labor.

1667 • The number of blacks on English sugar plantations on the Caribbean island of Barbados reaches 40,000, nearly twice the number of whites.

1670 • Virginia passes a law prohibiting blacks from owning indenture contracts on whites, an indication of growing white fear of the increasing black population.

1674 • The Royal African Company begins shipping captured Africans directly from African Guinea to the American mainland colonies, initiating a large-scale slave trade.

1690–94 • The ratio of slaves to indentured servants in the colonies rises to 14 to 1 as black slavery rapidly replaces indentured servitude as a source of cheap labor.

1691 • A new Virginia law dictates the banishment of any white person who marries a black, mulatto, or Indian.

1696 • South Carolina passes the Act for the Better Ordering and Governing of Negroes and Slaves, a comprehensive code for regulating blacks.

1698 • England's Parliament ends the Royal African Company's monopoly on the slave trade. Many more entrepreneurs enter the trade, leading to stiff competition and cheaper prices for slaves.

1700–10 • As the slave trade expands, more than twice as many Africans arrive in colonial America as in the entire previous century.

1710 • Wealthy Virginia planter William Byrd records in his diary that, upon coming home late and finding himself locked out of his house, he beat his black servant for not waiting up for him.

1712 • Twenty-five blacks stage an uprising in New York City, burning buildings and killing nine whites. The rebels are later caught and executed as an example to other would-be slave insurgents.

1720 • South Carolina planters uncover a plot by a group of slaves to escape and kill whites. The planters burn and hang the plot's ringleaders.

1739 • Approximately 20 slaves at Stono, a plantation outside of Charleston, South Carolina, steal guns and gunpowder and head south, burning buildings and killing white people along the way. Joined by about 60 more slaves, "they call out Liberty" and fight for their freedom. As many as 25 whites and 50 blacks are killed before the militia quells the uprising. At least 250 such slave rebellions or conspiracies occur during the 1700s.

1750 • The proportion of slaves in Maryland society reaches one-third of the general population, escalating the already existing white fear of slave uprisings.

1770
- A free black man, Crispus Attucks, is shot by British soldiers in the infamous Boston Massacre, becoming the first American casualty of the American Revolution.
- Benjamin Banneker, a free black who had become a leading American intellectual, assists in surveying the site of present-day Washington, D.C.; 20 years later, Banneker begins writing a farmers' almanac, the first scientific work published by an African American.

1773
- A group of Boston blacks petitions the Massachusetts legislature for their freedom and an end to the breaking up of slave families. The legislature ignores the petition.
- A black Christian church opens in South Carolina, reflecting the rapid growth of Christianity, the "white man's religion," among American blacks; many, however, still cling to their native African beliefs.
- The black slave poet Phillis Wheatley publishes *Poems on Various Subjects, Religious and Moral*. Soon after the book appears, Wheatley's owners grant her freedom.

1775
- Paul Cuffe of Massachusetts, the wealthy black owner of a fleet of merchant ships, refuses to pay taxes levied by Congress to finance the American Revolution until blacks are granted the right to vote. Cuffe will eventually become a leader of the movement to free blacks and send them to colonize Africa.

1778
- A black regiment fights at the Battle of Rhode Island, afterward receiving the accolade that it "distinguished itself by deeds of desperate valor." Black soldiers fight alongside whites in every major battle of the American Revolution.

1783
- Massachusetts grants the right to vote to all free black adult males, largely as a result of protests initiated by Paul Cuffe.

1784
- Prince Hall, a black Methodist minister and revolutionary war veteran, receives a charter to found the first black Masonic lodge in America.

1

SUGAR REVOLUTION:
THE SLAVE TRADE
DEVELOPS

BY the time colonial America started buying and selling captured Africans, black slavery had become an institution in the Spanish and Portuguese colonies in South America and the Caribbean islands. And before slavery reached the New World at all, it had been developing and expanding for centuries. As early as the 9th century, the Arabs of northern Africa were shipping thousands of blacks each year from the fertile lands south of the Sahara desert to the slave markets of the Middle East. Some 500 years later, when Europeans began exploring the world, they, too, entered the market of human souls; using captured blacks, they set out to exploit the newly discovered lands on the far side of the Atlantic. During these centuries, as the slave trade grew and spread, whites came to regard blacks as somehow less than human, a view that seemed to justify their enslavement.

In adopting slavery, colonial Americans tapped into this well-established system of slaveholding prac-

Slave traders seize an African man as his wife and child look on in horror. Far from beginning in the New World, black slavery had been perpetrated for centuries by Europeans, Arabs, and Africans themselves.

Roped together at the neck, Egyptian slaves run to serve their master, Pharaoh Ramses II. The runners' image, carved more than 3,000 years ago, was discovered at Abu Simbel, the great temple the pharaoh built on the Nile River.

tices and attitudes. They took advantage of an institution that, to many whites at the time, seemed effective, natural, and morally acceptable. Thus, to understand how and why slavery took firm root in America, it is essential first to understand how the exploitation of African blacks became so systematic, widespread, and accepted in both the Old and New Worlds.

Before the 9th century, the institution of slavery was widespread but not associated with specific races or ethnic groups. Most slaves were war captives; in Europe as in Africa, the victors of a conflict routinely enslaved their defeated opponents. Whites enslaved whites; blacks enslaved blacks. A slave was expected to do the bidding of his or her master because the act of conquest had established the master's superior strength. Thus, the prevailing view was that slaves, regardless of skin color and ethnicity, were persons of lesser strength and legal status.

This view began to change, however, in the years following the creation of a vast Muslim empire in the 7th and 8th centuries. Adhering to the religious doctrines of the prophet Muhammad, Muslim Arab armies conquered lands from the Persian Gulf in the Middle East, across northern Africa, and into what is now southern Spain. The Arabs built a high culture that included large cities, magnificent palaces, complex political systems and laws, and centers of learning that produced fine literature and scientific knowledge.

As the Muslim empire expanded, it came into contact with the less advanced black cultures south of the Sahara. The Arabs looked on these cultures as inferior to their own. More important, they began to correlate this perceived inferiority with difference in skin color, deciding that because the blacks had a less advanced type of culture, they must be less advanced as a race. Thus, when they sought slave laborers—Islamic law forbade Muslims to enslave one another—they looked toward black Africa. A lucrative slave trade grew rapidly as Arab slavers captured blacks in both eastern and western Africa and exported them to the Middle East and other Arab lands. As historian John B. Boles explains in his study of slavery, *Black Southerners*,

> Black slaves were increasingly forced into . . . back-breaking labor in the salt and copper mines of North Africa and the sugarcane plantations of Egypt and southern Iraq. Blackness now came to be synonymous with slavery as the original Arabic word for slave, *abd*, evolved to mean simply a black man. A substantial market for African slaves outside Africa . . . had arisen, and concurrently the African had acquired the image of the natural slave. Both developments were to prove significant for initial European encounters with Africa and subsequently for the New World slave systems.

A sword-waving Arab officer directs a column of war prisoners headed for servitude. Although their religion forbade them to enslave other Muslims, Arab slavers felt free to prey on anyone who did not accept the doctrines of the prophet Muhammad.

Ironically, blacks participated in the Arab trade in black slaves. This self-contradictory situation started toward the end of the 11th century, when the Islamic faith began to spread beyond the Arab lands' southern borders and into sub-Saharan Africa. In 1086, for example, King Umme Jilne of the West African nation of Kanem-Bornu converted to Islam. Jilne began to establish close ties with Arab states to the north, even encouraging his people to make pilgrimages to the city of Mecca, Islam's spiritual capital. A later Kanemite king, Idris Alooma, made the pilgrimage himself and set up hostels in Mecca

for black pilgrims. He also built mosques (Muslim houses of worship) in Kanem and instituted Muslim social and moral reforms, including strict laws against adultery and obscenity.

As Muslims, the Kanemites were safe from enslavement by the Arab Muslims to the north. Indeed, Kanem became so closely tied to the Arabs that its residents readily supplied Arab slavers with black captives, prisoners of war taken in Kanem's raids on its non-Muslim southern neighbors. Although the captives were of the same race, the Kanemites viewed them as inferior because they were not Muslims. Thus Kanem, under Idris Alooma and other leaders, became part of the trans-Saharan slave pipeline that carried countless thousands of native Africans to servitude in strange, faraway lands.

For a few hundred years the black slave trade remained for the most part an exclusively Arab enterprise. In Europe slavery was not as widespread as in Arab lands, mainly because of the European feudal system. Feudal lords, usually well-to-do landowners, relied for labor on their serfs, tenant farmers who worked the land in exchange for the lords' protection. The relatively few slaves were still war captives whose status was defined by such factors as nationality or religion rather than race. For instance, Christians commonly enslaved Muslims and vice versa. Such captives more than filled Europe's limited needs for slave labor.

Eventually, however, the decline of feudalism and new and vigorous economic growth in many parts of Europe stimulated a desire for increased slave labor. In the 14th century the prosperous Italian kingdom of Genoa became the first European state to recognize the potential of the black slave trade. After studying the Arabs' profitable sugarcane markets, Genoese merchants became eager to establish sugarcane plantations on the Mediterranean island of Cyprus. An important key to the Arabs' success appeared to be their large-scale use of relatively cheap black slaves. Following the Arabs' lead, the Genoese began importing large numbers of blacks, within a few decades creating a thriving sugar industry that greatly expanded the European sugar market. In the process, the idea that blacks were inferior and natural slaves transferred itself to Europe.

The Portuguese, who soon became maritime and economic rivals of the Genoese, now began to seek their own share of the lucrative sugar market. In the early 1400s Portuguese navigators outfitted their ships with the triangular lanteen sail, an innovation borrowed from the Arabs. This new technology made the ships maneuverable in winds blowing from any direction, allowing the Portuguese to master the complex wind patterns of the islands and coasts of western Africa. The Muslims called these coasts *Bilad Ghana,* or "land of wealth," because many of the area's natives traded both ivory and gold. Careless pronunciation by European sailors soon twisted Bilad Ghana into "Guinea," the name that western Africa would bear for centuries to come.

Soon after Portugal mastered African waters, Portuguese slavers began raiding Guinea and taking black captives. At first the slavers brought most of these slaves back to Portugal, where they became laborers on sugar plantations as well as household servants and other kinds of workers. In the mid-1400s Gomez de Azurara, who worked for the Portuguese royal court, wrote his *Chronicle of the Discovery and Conquest of Guinea,* in which he described the first Africans brought to Portugal. According to Azurara,

> They never more tried to fly [flee], but rather in time forgot all about their own country. They were very loyal and

obedient servants, without malice. . . . After they began to use clothing they were for the most part very fond of display, so that they took great delight in robes of showy colors, and such was their love of finery that they picked up the rags that fell from the coats of other people of the country and sewed them on their own crude garments, taking great pleasure in these, as though it were matter of some greater Perfection.

The Portuguese branch of the slave trade continued to expand. In the 1450s Portuguese investors set up large Genoese-style sugarcane plantations on Madeira and the Canary Islands, located off the coast of northwestern Africa. At first the slave workforce consisted primarily of native islanders and Muslim war

A slave merchant shows his wares—a father and son— to a prospective buyer in a North African marketplace. Before the 9th century, slaves were most often captured and sold by people of their own race.

captives. But when these prisoners declined in numbers due to disease and other factors, the planters began importing black slaves, some directly from Africa and others who had already been "broken in" on plantations in Portugal.

Shortly before 1500 Portugal opened a huge sugarcane industry on Sao Thomé, an island on the equator about 200 miles off the African coast. Because of the large number of slaves used and massive amounts of sugar produced, the Sao Thomé venture constituted the height of the European-African slave system. The island's industry was also significant in that it used almost exclusively slaves imported directly from the West African coast. Sao Thomé's design, operation, and slave system became the chief model for the Caribbean plantations that would soon follow.

The Spanish organized the first of these New World sugarcane industries on the island of Hispaniola, east of Cuba, and began importing African slaves in 1502. At first black slavery grew slowly in the area, largely because the Spanish plantations were not immediately successful. Their early failure to prosper resulted from the Spaniards' shifting of their resources and energies into exploiting the gold and other treasures reportedly possessed by the natives of Central America. Also, Spanish planters initially felt it was more economical to enslave these natives than to import blacks from across the ocean. Because of limited Spanish sugar production, later in the century the enterprising Portuguese managed to capture the New World sugar market. Portugal built a large-scale sugarcane industry in Brazil, which by 1600 was known as the world's "sugar bowl." As in the past, the Portuguese system relied heavily on black slaves imported directly from Africa.

In the first few decades of the 17th century the sugar industry, which had been growing slowly but steadily for centuries, suddenly exploded in size, scope, and profitability. And the black slave trade, which supplied the labor that was the backbone of this industry, grew in corresponding measure. One reason for this "sugar revolution" was that rising populations and standards of living in Europe increased demands for the substance. In turn, the huge mass production that ensued made sugar more affordable and stimulated demand still further.

The Portuguese, Spanish, and Dutch all vied for shares of the exploding sugar market. And England and France, whose New World economic interests had previously been confined largely to the North American mainland, also rushed to acquire pieces of the market. The English established their first sugar colony on Barbados in 1627. Various European nations followed suit on other Caribbean islands, including Jamaica, St. Croix, Guadeloupe, and San Domingo. The vast wealth produced by the plantations on these "sugar islands" helped finance the worldwide empires that England and other European powers built in the following century. All this economic growth was made possible by the use of mass black slave labor.

The number of African slaves imported into the sugar islands was staggering. By 1643, only 16 years after first colonizing Barbados, the English had already imported some 6,000 blacks; by 1667 that number had grown to 40,000, nearly twice the number of whites on the island. Other Caribbean islands also imported and exploited large numbers of blacks. On Jamaica, for example, the slave population grew from only a few hundred in 1655 to nearly 211,000 in 1787. Of the estimated total of 12 million Africans brought in chains to the New World between

Twenty captured Africans, the first blacks to enter the New World, arrive at Jamestown, Virginia, in 1619. The shipment inaugurated almost 250 years of American slavery.

1450 and 1870, fully half went to the sugar islands and at least another 25 percent to Portuguese sugar plantations in Brazil.

The English colonies on the American mainland were the last New World settlements to take advantage of the well-established African slave trade. Even after they began importing slaves, these colonies did so much more slowly and on a far smaller scale than did the sugar island colonies. "It was in the backwash of this dynamic Caribbean sugar boom," John Boles points out, "that slavery developed on the North American mainland." As late as 1615, when Spain and Portugal were regularly exploiting Africans in all their New World colonies, the North American colonies, partly because their climate was not amenable to growing sugar, had no black slaves at all. Then, in 1619, as scholar J. Saunders Redding describes it in his book *They Came in Chains*, a ship made a fateful landing at Jamestown in the English colony of Virginia:

> Sails furled, flag drooping at her rounded stern, she rode the tide in from the sea. She was a strange ship, indeed. . . . Whether she was a trader, privateer, or man-of-war no one knows. . . . She came, she traded, and shortly afterwards was gone. Probably no ship in modern history has carried a more portentous freight. Her cargo? Twenty slaves.

2

"FELLOW SUFFERERS":
EARLY COLONIAL SLAVERY

A T first black slavery developed slowly in colonial America. Too far north for sugarcane cultivation, the mainland colonies were small in size and scope and had no need for the large-scale labor forces employed in Brazil and the Caribbean. Moreover, most American settlers initially came to the New World to find religious and political freedom rather than for economic gain. They fully expected to build their own houses and work their own fields, to be self-sufficient while freely practicing their beliefs. However, the eventual introduction of tobacco and other valuable cash crops in America established new labor needs. Colonists in Jamestown, Virginia, founded in 1607, for example, realized that they could not become economically prosperous without extra workers. And it seemed only natural at the time to tap into the black slave trade so well established by the sugar industry to the south.

Slaves process tobacco leaves on a 17th-century Virginia plantation. Probably based only on verbal reports, this British engraving includes a fanciful tree, a tobacco plant (left), and a turkey, a creature the English considered quintessentially American.

Closely watched by a whip-bearing overseer, blacks gather sugarcane in Brazil. Because sugar cultivation took a heavy toll on the slaves who made it possible, South American and Caribbean planters imported huge numbers of captive Africans.

Originally, the American colonists intended to use imported blacks merely to supplement a mostly white workforce. They did not envision basing their economy on slave labor, as in the sugar islands, and as a result their early attitude toward blacks was completely unlike that of the sugar planters. During the first few decades of black slavery in America, slaves were few in number and not perceived by whites as a threat. Whites often worked alongside blacks in Virginia and elsewhere, and a number of slaves earned their freedom and enjoyed many of the rights whites did. The status of blacks was higher than it would be later, when slavery had become widely practiced and deeply rooted.

Had the North American colonists been able to enslave American Indian laborers—as some other early New World explorers had done—they might never have started to supplement their workforce with black workers. But the mainland American settlers found the Indians to be extremely self-reliant and difficult to exploit. As Howard Zinn puts it in *A People's History of the United States,* the colonists

> were outnumbered, and while, with superior firearms, they could massacre Indians, they would face massacre in return. They could not capture them and keep them enslaved; the Indians were tough, resourceful, defiant, and at home in these woods, as the transplanted Englishmen were not. . . . There may have been a kind of frustrated rage at their own ineptitude, at the Indian superiority at taking care of themselves, that made the Virginians especially ready to become the masters of slaves.

To the colonists, it seemed far easier to enslave blacks. First, they did not have to go to the trouble of searching out and capturing blacks, as they did Indians. Africans came to the New World already in chains, physically controlled and psychologically disoriented. Unlike the Indians, black slaves had been torn from their native lands and thrust into an unfamiliar and frightening environment. Left on their own, they would have found it as difficult as whites did to survive. For most blacks it seemed preferable to labor obligingly for their white masters than to escape and face death by starvation or an Indian hatchet. Buying African slaves, then, seemed to the settlers the most efficient way to supplement their own white workforce.

Nevertheless, in the years following the arrival of the first 20 black slaves in Jamestown in 1619, slavery developed very slowly in North America. The colonists had carried with them a decided prejudice against non-English ways; because few Englishmen owned slaves, few colonists wished to do so. Those who did buy slaves acted out of what they saw as necessity rather than out of preference.

Women peel potatoes and churn butter in a colonial kitchen. In their early years in America, English settlers relied for their labor needs on white indentured servants—people who agreed to work for a fixed period in exchange for transportation to the New World.

The early settlers much preferred the well-established European system of indentured servitude. An indentured servant was a landless or otherwise impoverished individual who voluntarily signed a work contract with a person of means. The servant promised to work a specific number of years for that person in return for land, money, or some other reward. Indentured servitude thus involved the temporary ownership of a person's labor, rather than the permanent ownership of the actual person. Many of the American colonies' indentured servants were Englishmen who committed themselves to several years of work in exchange for passage across the Atlantic.

These people needed no training in English labor methods and, because their service was voluntary, required no restraints.

Another reason for slavery's slow growth in the colonies was the nature of the settlers' farming. They began with corn and other food crops, but in 1612 Virginian John Rolfe began to experiment with a new plant: tobacco. Finding that the aromatic leaf grew well in the area, he continued to cultivate it, soon shipping a batch to London. Smoking quickly became popular, and a thriving market for American tobacco was born. By 1617 demand for the product was so great that Jamestown's inhabitants were said to be growing it in the streets. But because tobacco required a much smaller labor force per acre than did sugarcane, planters could take advantage of the tobacco boom without abandoning their reliance on white indentured servants. Between 1620 and 1660, such workers remained the backbone of the large colonial farms, and planters imported few African slaves. In 1625, for example, more than 10 years into the colonial tobacco boom, the Virginia colony's census listed only 23 blacks. And even as late as the mid-1650s, only a few hundred blacks lived in the tidewater area, the rich coastal plain where the colonies of Virginia and Maryland had developed.

Still another reason for slavery's slow development in early colonial America was that Englishmen at the time were uncomfortable living and working around non-English peoples. This coolness extended to a wide range of nationalities and groups, including the Irish, the Spanish and Portuguese, and the local Indians. With language and cultural roots decidedly alien to the English, African blacks were, not surprisingly, also the targets of such prejudice. Yet in the beginning the settlers' negative feelings toward blacks were based more on fear and distrust of unknown ways and ideas than on intolerance of different skin color. For the

John Rolfe, a 25-year-old Englishman who settled in Virginia in 1610, cultivates an experimental crop: tobacco. Sometimes called the father of the American tobacco industry, Rolfe sent a shipment of leaves to England in 1613, sparking an instant demand for the aromatic product.

most part, the early planters simply felt more comfortable around white indentured servants who shared their ethnic and cultural background. So they imported few blacks.

An indication that deep-rooted racism had not yet taken hold in the colonies was demonstrated by the free status of some blacks. A number of Africans served a set number of years and then gained their freedom, as indentured servants did. In 1668 in Vir-

ginia's Northampton County, some 29 percent of blacks were free. It is also significant that the majority of black workers who remained slaves for life were rarely segregated from indentured white workers, and were treated in substantially the same way.

"On southern plantations where white servants worked alongside Negro slaves," notes historian John C. Miller in *The First Frontier: Life in Colonial America,* "they often did the same kind of work and put in the same number of hours in the field." Most planters neither spared whites the worst jobs nor automatically assigned these jobs to blacks. On many plantations, black and white workers bunked together, ate the same foods, and sometimes even had children to-gether with little or no social condemnation. As long as blacks remained few and scattered in colonial soci-ety, white workers generally looked upon them as fellow sufferers rather than as inferiors.

Thus two distinct groups of blacks existed in early colonial America: slave workers who received largely the same treatment as indentured white workers, and former slaves who had gained their freedom. In addi-tion to those who earned liberty after a set term of service, others were freed because they were the prod-ucts of mixed marriages. In such cases a white father's legal status ensured that his children, regardless of race, could not be enslaved. Other blacks borrowed money from their masters, used it to purchase their freedom, and then paid back the debt in the following years. Still others sought and gained their freedom in the courts. Some argued successfully that they had labored faithfully for a fair term of service and de-served, like indentured whites, to be rewarded for that service.

That blacks were allowed to petition the courts at all reflected the relatively broad legal status they enjoyed at the time. Free blacks could not only sue in court but also serve on juries and testify against whites.

They also had the right to own land. Between 1664 and 1677 in Northampton County, for instance, at least 13 of the county's 101 blacks became free land-owners. Blacks also owned livestock and other kinds of property. They could and sometimes did own black slaves, and a few black farmers even had white inden-tured servants. Virginia did not pass a law forbidding blacks from owning indenture contracts on whites until 1670. And some blacks took out loans, paid taxes, held minor public office, and occasionally, in colonies that allowed it, even voted. Thus, in colonial America's first few decades, both law and custom worked to moderate both racial prejudice and the cruel fact of slavery.

Widespread English prejudice against anyone non-English, however, provided for some impor-tant distinctions. The local tax laws offer a clear illustration. According to a 1649 statute, only male inhabitants "of all sorts above 16 years of age"—including free black men—were required to pay taxes. Women of all races were exempt from taxation. Later, however, as English feel-ings of cultural superiority surfaced with increas-ing frequency, colonial lawmakers appeared uncomfortable with allowing black women the same privileges as white women. One way to make a distinction was to eliminate the special tax exemption. A law passed in 1668 requiring free black women to pay taxes stated,

> Whereas some doubts have arisen whether negro women set free were still to be exempt [from taxation] according to a former act, it is declared by this grand assembly [Virginia's legislature] that negro women, though per-mitted to enjoy their freedom yet ought not in all re-spects to be admitted to a full fruition [enjoyment] of the exemptions and impunities of the English, and are still liable to the payment of taxes.

The relatively lenient treatment of black slaves, including the opportunity to gain both freedom and a broad array of legal rights, was short-lived. In the mid-to-late 1600s sweeping economic and social changes began to transform the way blacks lived. As the once-uncommon and scattered occurrence of slavery grew relentlessly into a widespread and entrenched institution, treatment of black workers would worsen and the legal status of all blacks would fall.

3

FROM A TRICKLE
TO A FLOOD

ENGLISH prosperity sharply reduced the flow of indentured servants to America after 1660. To deal with the colonies' resulting labor shortage, planters began to buy more African slaves, increasing the ratio of blacks to whites. A mere trickle in the mid-1660s, the tide of incoming blacks had become a virtual flood by the 1690s. In his book *American Slavery*, historian Peter Kolchin notes that

> at the same time that colonial demand for labor was surging, a sharp *decrease* occurred in the number of English migrants arriving in America under indenture. White immigration into the tidewater colonies—most of it indentured—peaked between 1650 and 1680 and then declined sharply. In some areas the decline was dramatic. In York County, Virginia, for example, the ratio of servants to slaves plummeted from 1.9/1 [about two servants for each slave] in 1680–84 to 0.27/1 [four slaves for each servant] in 1685–89 and 0.07/1 [14 slaves for each servant] in 1690–94; within a decade, indentured servants had almost totally disappeared from the country.

Surrounded by curious townspeople, an auctioneer takes bids for a black man in 1643. At this point, Africans were still something of a novelty in the American colonies, but a few decades later they would constitute a significant part of the population, especially in the South.

Under a flaming sky, Londoners flee in terror during the city's Great Fire of 1666. Rebuilding after the conflagration, which destroyed 13,200 houses, opened up a huge job market, reducing the number of workers eager to indenture themselves as American servants.

This sudden decline in white plantation workers—which, in turn, increased the demand for black slaves—stemmed from a mix of economic and geographic factors. Among them was a sharp downturn in England's birthrate, caused partly by the civil war that racked the nation in the 1640s. Because fewer children were born during this period, there were fewer adults around to become indentured in the 1680s. Also, the 1660s saw a general rise in wages and job opportunities in England. For example, large numbers of people found employment rebuilding London after the Great Fire of 1666. Not surprisingly, therefore, fewer people felt the need to seek work in the colonies. During the latter part of the 1600s the Carolinas, Pennsylvania, New Hampshire, and other eastern areas experienced rapid settlement. With more destinations to choose among, the dwindling number of indentured Britons who did emigrate to America headed for plantation country.

In the colonists' eyes, slaves held several advantages over white servants. First, slavery gave the master a reliable labor source over which he had almost complete control. White servants often ran away, but blacks could, because of their color, be quickly identified, making their escape far less likely. Whites earned their liberty, after which they might rise in wealth and position, competing with their former masters; such a scenario was unavailable to blacks. Finally, slaves were cheaper; a master did not have to free them with money and land, as he did a white servant who had completed his contract.

The transition from indentured to slave labor in the colonies seemed morally justified to most Englishmen. Although a handful of individuals protested, as they have in every age, insisting that it was wrong for one person to own another, the vast majority of whites accepted the concept of slavery as the natural way of things. After all, they asserted, throughout history the weak had always done the bidding of the strong. And there was no doubt in the average Englishman's mind that English ways were superior to those of other peoples, especially peoples who were less technically advanced.

Whites further justified slavery by suggesting that a slave's standard of living was no worse than that of a poor Englishman. In his *Reminiscences of an American Loyalist,* colonial minister Jonathan Boucher summed up this view:

> Negroes in Virginia and Maryland . . . were not upon the whole worse off nor less happy than the laboring poor in Great Britain. . . . I have known thousands of slaves as well-informed, as well-clad, as well-fed, and in every respect as well off as nine out of ten of the poor in every kingdom of Europe are. Nor is the possession of slaves so desirable an acquisition as may be imagined: if a wrong be done to them, as I question not there is, in making them slaves, their owners are probably sufficiently punished by the unpleasant nature of their services.

The rapid increase in slave imports from both the Caribbean and Africa's Guinea Coast in the late 1600s occurred mainly in Virginia and Maryland. The Carolinas, which had been settled later than the tidewater colonies, did not begin large-scale importation of slaves until the early 1700s. And in the northern colonies—especially those in New England, where no significant plantation economy had developed—slavery never became an important part of the economy.

The increases in Virginia's black population were dramatic. According to the colony's census records, out of a total population of some 15,000 in 1649, only about 300, or 2 percent, were blacks. Twenty-two years later, in 1671, the number of blacks in Virginia had risen to 2,000, 5 percent of the colony's total population of 40,000. And by 1700 Virginia had approximately 16,000 blacks, more than 30 percent of the overall population, the vast majority of them slaves for life. Maryland, a smaller colony, had fewer inhabitants, but its ratio of blacks to whites was similar to Virginia's.

Another reason for the sharp increase in the importation of slaves was direct English involvement in the African slave trade. Prior to the early 1600s, Portugal and Spain had dominated the trade. Through its increasing naval superiority in the mid-to-late 1600s, however, England gained control of a significant portion of the Atlantic shipping market and with

Working as a team, slaves raise their voices in song while they harvest cotton. Many whites insisted that the lives led by enslaved African Americans were as pleasant as those of poor English people; in the mid-1600s this assertion had some validity, but blacks' living standards dropped sharply as the century drew to a close.

it a major share of the lucrative slave trade. In 1674 the Royal African Company, an English corporation established two years earlier, began shipping slaves directly from Guinea to the mainland American colonies. As the company delivered increasing numbers of Africans, the market expanded and the price per slave decreased somewhat. Many planters in the tidewater region took advantage of reduced prices and bought more slaves.

For a time, the Royal African Company held a virtual monopoly on the West African slave trade. Initially headed by England's powerful duke of York, the company received its official

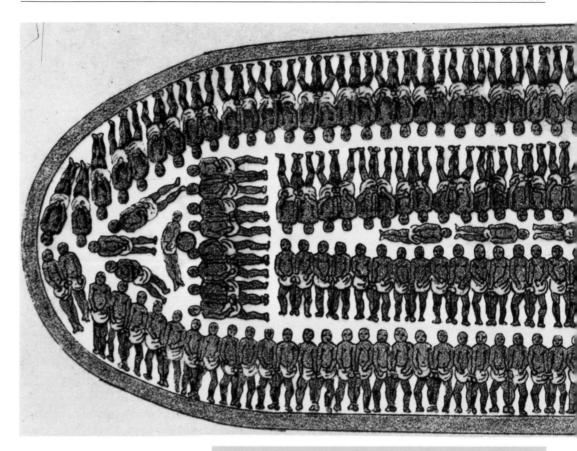

charter, or legal authorization to operate, from Parliament in 1672. The English legislative body gave the company sole rights to plunder the African coast from Morocco in the north to the Cape of Good Hope, some 5,000 miles to the south. Start-up money for the Royal African came from private English citizens. These investors—people who owned no plantations and may never even have seen an African—not only helped create and support the slave trade but made a handsome profit while they were at it.

The company, which sold some 2,000 slaves a year in Jamaica alone, frequently offered its customers special deals. For example, as scholar

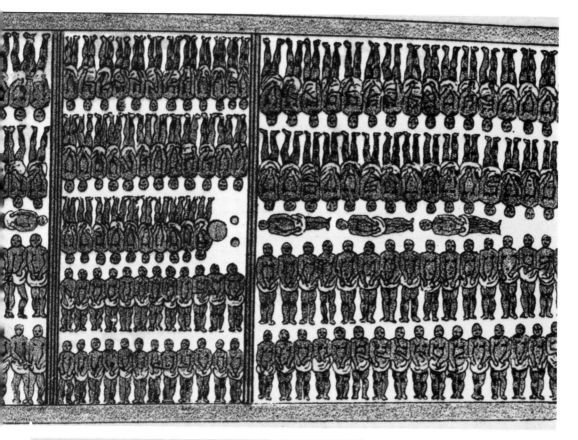

Crammed into the lower deck of a "guineaman," or slave ship, captured Africans face weeks of foul air, skimpy rations, and almost no space to move. Passengers on one of these "tight pack" slavers stood an even chance of dying before the voyage from Africa to America ended.

The cost of slaves dropped sharply after 1698, when Parliament ended the Royal African Company's monopoly. Now almost any enterprising Englishman with money to hire a ship and crew could enter the slave trade. Many did so, creating a climate of cut-throat competition that reduced the price of slaves still further. Increasing the demand for this human merchandise was the planters' realization that buying two slaves, a man and a woman, provided an added benefit: the pair might produce offspring whom the master would already own, a bonus on his original investment. As a result of these factors, the number of North American slave imports rose briskly in the first decade of the 18th century. Between 1700 and 1710 more than twice as many Africans arrived in colonial America as in the entire previous century.

As blacks became more prevalent in the colonies, many whites became disquieted by their number. Before, when slaves had been few and scattered, they had been relatively easy to regulate and control. Now there seemed a growing danger of slaves running away or even turning on their masters. Even more disturbing to some whites was the notion that a larger slave population would eventually produce more free blacks. Living among whites and competing for white jobs, these free men and women might employ white workers, socialize with whites, and even marry them.

Whites also noticed that as blacks' presence increased, they tended to identify culturally more with one another than with whites. When they had been few in number, black workers had tended to adopt many of their white coworkers' ways. This allowed blacks, at least to some degree, to seem part of white society, making them more acceptable to whites. Now, surrounded by more members of their own race, blacks were better able to retain aspects of their own African cultures. All these factors contributed to a growing perception among whites in the late 1600s that blacks posed a potential threat to white society.

White society responded to the perceived threat by passing laws specifically denying blacks certain rights and tightening the grip of slaveholders on their human property. One of the first such laws, a statute passed in Virginia in 1662, disallowed "mulattoes" (the offspring of mixed marriages) the right to gain freedom on the grounds that their fathers were white. "Whereas some doubts have arisen whether children got by any Englishman upon a negro woman shall be slave or free," the law stated, "all children born in this colony shall be bond or free only according to the condition of the mother." As most black women were slaves, their children, regardless of the father's race, were now condemned to slavery too. Despite this law, some interracial marriages continued to occur. Most whites increasingly viewed this practice as socially unacceptable, and in 1691 Virginia enacted a law providing for the banishment of any "white man or woman being free who shall intermarry with a negro, mulatto, or Indian man or woman bond or free."

Other laws, too, strengthened the institution of slavery. In order to eliminate the then-common practice of freeing a slave after a set term of service, in 1664 Maryland passed a law mandating that all slaves must serve for life. Believing it wrong to enslave a Christian, masters had for years been freeing slaves who accepted baptism. In 1667 a Virginia statute eliminated this loophole, stipulating that baptism no longer altered a slave's condition. Three years later Virginia passed a law forbidding blacks to buy the contracts of white indentured servants. Other laws forbade slaves from carrying weapons, leaving home without written permission from their masters, or challenging white authority in any way. Freed blacks, too, felt the weight of oppressive new laws. No longer, for example, could a free black person vote or testify in court against a white person.

Some colonies enacted comprehensive slave codes that covered all aspects of black-white relations. South Carolina's code, passed in 1696 and entitled *Act for the Better Ordering and Governing of Negroes and*

Alabama field hands pick cotton in the mid-1700s. By this time, southern states had passed a series of "black codes," rigid laws that aimed at controlling blacks' "barbarous, wild, savage nature" by depriving them of almost all human rights.

Slaves, was typical. The document's preface stated in part:

> Whereas, the plantations and estates of this Province cannot be well and sufficiently managed and brought into use, without the labor and service of negroes and other slaves [Indians]; and as forasmuch as the said negroes and other slaves brought into the people of this Province for that purpose, are of barbarous, wild, savage natures, and such as renders them wholly unqualified to be governed by the laws, customs and practices of this Province . . . it is absolutely necessary, that such other . . . laws and orders . . . be made and enacted, for the good of regulating and ordering of them.

Such laws did more than lower blacks' social and legal status. The changing attitudes and practices of whites regarding blacks in general and slavery in particular in the last decades of the 18th century prepared the way for a new economic and social way of life in the American South. It would be a society built almost entirely upon the backs of enslaved Africans.

4

PLANTATION BOOM

AS planters' labor demands intensified and the African slave trade expanded, southern colonists put the finishing touches on their "black codes"—the harsh laws they designed to protect themselves from their black "property." What these colonists had created by the first decade of the 18th century was a new and radically different society; no longer guided by the pioneer spirit of determined personal effort, theirs had become a world based on the sweat and blood and bones of others. Historian Peter Kolchin describes that world:

> The colonial era saw the emergence in America of a true slave society, the transformation of a society in which some people (relatively few, at first) were slaves into one in which slave labor formed the basis of the economy and social order. . . . Gradually, social patterns hardened: as masters and slaves were born into slave relations, behavior that had once been tentative and experimental became established and routine.

Montpelier, the 5,000-acre Virginia estate of James Madison, was home not only to the future president (he would serve as chief executive from 1809 to 1817) but to about 100 enslaved African Americans. Madison liked to boast that his slaves' labor produced far more income than he spent in feeding and housing them.

47

*An 18th-century engraving shows a tobacco plant (*tabac *in French, nicotiana *in Latin*) dominating the Virginia countryside.*

Although tobacco required fewer workers per acre, its culture, especially in the early colonial years, had an important effect on the development of the South's large-scale slave economy. The huge success of tobacco established land—specifically plantations, along with the methods, livestock, and slaves that supported them—as the main source of money and status for white southerners. According to historian John Miller,

> In Virginia and Maryland, the profits made in agriculture tended to be ploughed back into the land, slaves, and the amenities of life. Until the middle of the 18th century, the cultivation of tobacco was so profitable that it absorbed almost all the energy and capital of the Chesapeake [tidewater] planters. In consequence, land became the honorific form of wealth: it conferred social esteem and political power.

In the southern colonies in the 1700s, the larger a man's plantation, the higher was his standard of living, social status, and local influence. An extended plantation, whether it produced tobacco, rice, or cotton, of course required more slaves to operate. It is not surprising, then, that the demand for slaves increased and that the economy came to depend on them.

The plantation economy was successful partly because an owner was able to make a huge return on his investment in a slave. The initial money spent on the purchase was small in light of the fact that the owner could get 20 to 40—or even more—years of labor from the slave. And slaves were relatively inexpensive to house and feed. In the late colonial period, American patriot and slave owner James Madison told a visitor that he spent only $12 or $13 per year on upkeep for each of his slaves. Yet, Madison boasted, he made some $257 per year from the labor of each of those slaves.

Making slaves even more profitable were the long days they could be forced to labor: a workday of 13 to 15 hours was common. To make sure that their plantations ran smoothly and that their slaves worked diligently, many owners lived on their plantations. Often with the aid of overseers, the most successful

Barefoot slaves pick cotton in Georgia. Here and in neighboring South Carolina, some plantation owners employed the "task system," believing that slaves who regulated their own work produced far more than those who were closely supervised.

planters supervised their slaves closely, also keeping a sharp eye on all the other aspects of farm operation. This set American planters apart from their European counterparts, who rarely or never visited their plantations in the Caribbean and Brazil.

Although most of the South's planters lived on their estates, the practice was by no means universal. Some of the wealthiest owners, disliking the hard work, tedium, and day-to-day realities of farm life, spent most of their time in the cities. The coastal lowlands of South Carolina and Georgia, where plantations were larger and wealthier than those in most other parts of the South, had the most absentee owners. These planters developed what became known as the "task system," a program in which each slave received a work assignment in the morning. He or she was allowed to stop work when the task was finished, even if it had taken only a few hours. Kolchin notes that

> absentee planters often allowed their . . . slaves an unusual degree of self-management, with estates left in the hands of trusted black "drivers" who were in effect overseers, and who operated under the loose control of white "stewards," each of whom supervised several estates. . . . Along the coast of South Carolina and Georgia . . . slaves developed their own "internal economy" based on flexible work schedules and the ability to accumulate and dispose of their "own" property on their "own" time.

Absentee planters defended the task system, asserting that it gave slaves a powerful incentive to work. But the majority of southern planters disagreed; they believed that the system allowed slaves too much freedom and independence, thereby fostering a breakdown of discipline and order among slaves. For this reason, the task system never became widespread outside South Carolina and Georgia lowlands.

One revealing indicator of the new American slave economy's success was the rise in the number of slave imports during the 1700s. Of the estimated 650,000 Africans brought to America between 1619 and the 1860s, fully 60 percent, or some 390,000, arrived between 1720 and 1775. Also revealing are the black population increases for individual colonies. In Virginia the number of slaves rose from 16,000 in 1700, the beginning of the plantation boom, to 170,000—about half the colony's population—in 1763. And in Maryland the black population increased from 3,000 to 43,000 between 1700 and 1750.

The ever-mounting demand for slaves reflected the state of the economy: as the black workforce grew, crop exports and overall profits grew accordingly. The success of South Carolina's rice cultivation was typical of the South's economic picture. In 1724, the colony exported about 4,000 tons of rice. By 1749, yearly exports had climbed to 14,000 tons, and in 1765 they reached a staggering 32,000 tons (64 million pounds).

These numbers do not tell the whole story of the growth of colonial America's slave population and its effect on the economy. When a planter bought a slave, he acquired not only one lifetime of low-cost labor but the potential of several lifetimes, as he would also own the slave's offspring and descendants. By 1775, when the colonial period ended with the start of the American Revolution, more than twice as many blacks lived in the colonies as had been imported between 1700 and 1775. Clearly, black slaves reproduced rapidly during the second half of the colonial period.

The explosion in black birthrates during the 1700s was a phenomenon peculiar to America. Only 5 per-

Household slaves sweep the walks at Monticello, Thomas Jefferson's Virginia plantation. Jefferson, who tried to insert a passage condemning slavery into the Declaration of Independence, nevertheless owned almost 200 slaves.

cent of all the slaves brought to the New World between 1451 and 1870 ended up on North American shores, but because of these high birthrates, by 1825 36 percent of the New World's slaves lived in North America. By contrast, the birthrates of slaves in the Caribbean and other areas of the New World were so low that they resulted in decreases in black populations. The island of Jamaica, for example, imported more than 750,000 slaves during the centuries it participated in the slave trade. Yet in 1834, the year Jamaican slaves received emancipation, the island's black population numbered only 311,000.

Historians have given several reasons for 18th-century North America's high birthrates among blacks. One was that more of North America's female slaves survived the ordeal of slavery and bore children than the female slaves of the sugar colonies in the Caribbean and South America. The American plantation slaves lived and procreated because their working and living conditions, although far from ideal, were considerably more humane than on the sugar plantations farther south, where it was common practice for overseers to starve slaves and work them literally to death under a blazing sun. Also, disease epidemics were more common and more lethal on the tropical sugar plantations. John Boles explains,

> In Latin America and in the Caribbean, where the labor routines were far more harsh and the disease climate more severe, fewer African women survived long enough to bear children, and far fewer infants survived childhood. In the mainland colonies, however, even though the few children born of African women could not initially sustain the population, since they were equally divided by sex and grew up adjusted to the New World disease environment, they as adults would be significantly more fruitful than their parents. The key to potential black population growth, then, was the presence of a plantation environment where the normal work routines were reasonable enough, the food supply plentiful enough, and disease sufficiently under control to allow the initial African women to survive and produce children.

African women, however, rarely gave birth during their first years in North America. Traumatized by capture and the horrifying transatlantic voyage, many stopped menstruating, thereby becoming infertile for several years. Black women born in America, on the other hand, had normal reproductive cycles, and often began bearing children in their early teenage years.

The adoption by black women of a European custom also contributed significantly to accelerated black population growth. In Africa, mothers customarily breast-fed their children for two or three years; because women are far less likely to become pregnant while breast-feeding, African women's children usually arrived several years apart. European women, on the other hand, rarely breast-fed their infants for longer than one year; when the slave women followed this example, weaning their babies after 10 or 12 months, they often found themselves pregnant every year.

The first increases in the black birthrate had a snowball effect. First, with more blacks around, black men and women had better chances of choosing mates. Second, during these same years American settlers were building new roads and bridging rivers throughout the countryside, making travel and communication between plantations easier. Many blacks, with their masters' permission, met and married workers on neighboring plantations and formed dispersed, but nevertheless large, family groups. John Boles comments,

> On smaller plantations, males were able to visit their spouses on neighboring farms. [The slaves on successful plantations were rarely sold], and even when death or debts forced a sale, slaves were likely to be purchased by slaveholders who lived close by. These cumulative changes produced a more stable, less precarious life for typical slaves.

The slaves' permanent families, along with networks of friends and relatives, not only helped raise the birthrate and thereby boost the slave economy, but also contributed to a feeling of community among blacks. In this way, increased black population growth helped stimulate the emergence of African American culture.

The character of American slavery was shaped not only by rapid black population growth but by the way slaves were distributed across the colonial countryside. In the sugar islands, most plantations were huge, factory-like operations attended by hundreds, and often thousands, of slaves. In North America, the average planter could not afford to buy and maintain large gangs

of slaves. In the first three decades of the 18th century, more than half the tidewater planters owned five or fewer slaves; some owned more, but only a small minority had more than 50.

Planters who did own large numbers of slaves often divided them among different landholdings. Robert "King" Carter, who was probably Virginia's wealthiest man in the 1720s, owned some 400 slaves, but he also owned 48 separate properties, and he assigned some of his formidable workforce to each of them. The largest single group of Carter's slaves, 23 men and women, worked on his home plantation. In 1770 Carter's grandson, Robert Carter III, employed 100 slaves on his home plantation and kept 250 others scattered among his 12 other properties. And in 1774 future U.S. president Thomas Jefferson held 45 slaves at Monticello, the estate where he lived, and 142 more on six other farms. Dividing their slaves in this way allowed these planters to expand and diversify their holdings. Rich men thus grew richer.

5

FROM AFRICA TO AMERICA

SHIPS from the American colonies, England, and other countries brought more black slaves to America in the 18th century than at any other time. By the mid-1700s—the peak period of its prosperity—the transatlantic trade in human beings had become as profitable as the agricultural systems it supplied.

Just as 9th-century Africans had captured other Africans for the Arab slave trade, 18th-century Africans sold fellow blacks to the Europeans. At that time, an African might become a slave in one of several ways. Already the property of a West African tribe—most African tribes kept slaves—they might simply be traded to the whites, exchanging a black master for a white. Some of these slaves had been sentenced to servitude for committing a crime or being deeply in debt; others had been kidnapped from neighboring tribes. The majority, however, were prisoners of war taken in the frequent conflicts between neighboring tribes and kingdoms.

Ready to set sail from Africa to America, slavers brand a captive on the shoulder. Before they reached the African coastal markets, slaves were often forced to march hundreds of miles, an ordeal that killed about two in every five of them.

Musket-armed African guards oversee prisoners as they march toward the west coast of Africa. Blacks intended for the slave trade were rounded up by both white and black traders.

Because African tribal leaders and European slavers grew rich from dealing in human traffic, each side was careful to maintain good relations with the other. Historian John Boles comments,

> The Europeans paid the local chieftain an annual rent, purchased water and provisions from him, and depended upon him to supply them with slaves. The African chief or king sold his war captives, those of his own people enslaved for whatever reason, or victims captured by his agents deep in the interior [of the African continent] or bought "wholesale" at interior slave markets, for a whole spectrum of European goods ranging from gunpowder and cloth to iron bars and cowrie shells.

During the height of the 18th-century slave trade, white dealers and customers often justified slavery by pointing out that the Africans them-

selves owned slaves. African slavery, however, was decidedly different from New World slavery. Slaves in Africa sometimes received harsh treatment, but they also had certain basic rights never granted to the slaves of the Caribbean and American colonies. In Africa slaves could marry, own property (including their own slaves), and become heirs to their masters' property. A slave who remained with a family for life could and frequently did become an adopted member of that family, occasionally even marrying one of its members. For the most part, slaves performed regular family and village duties rather than relentless backbreaking toil. Describing some of the peoples living along the West African coast in the 1700s, John Newton of Liverpool, England—a slave trader who later experienced a religious conversion and became a minister and antislavery advocate—wrote,

> The state of slavery, among these wild barbarous people, as we esteem them, is much milder than in our colonies. For as, on the one hand, they have no land in high cultivation, like our West India [Caribbean] plantations, and therefore no call for that excessive, unintermitted labor, which exhausts our slaves; so, on the other hand, no man is permitted to draw blood even from a slave.

Modern scholar Howard Zinn sums up the contrasts between the African and American versions of slavery:

> African slavery is hardly to be praised. But it was far different from plantation or mining slavery in the Americas, which was . . . morally crippling, destructive of family ties, without hope of any future. African slavery lacked . . . the reduction of the slave to less than human status by the use of racial hatred, with that relentless clarity based on color, where white was master, black was slave.

In the next phase of the captured blacks' induction into lifelong servitude, white slavers or African mid-

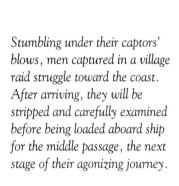
Stumbling under their captors' blows, men captured in a village raid struggle toward the coast. After arriving, they will be stripped and carefully examined before being loaded aboard ship for the middle passage, the next stage of their agonizing journey.

dlemen marched them, usually shackled around the neck, overland to the beaches of West Africa, where the slave ships periodically anchored. When the slaves came from areas near the coast, these journeys were relatively short. In other cases the slavers moved the captives hundreds of miles through all kinds of terrain and weather, prodding them on with whips and guns. An estimated two out of every five of the people on these marches never made it to the beaches.

When the surviving Africans reached the beaches, they waited in cages until selected by the slave ship captains or other white middlemen. During this phase, the captives underwent their first forced physical examination. An eyewitness, John Barbot, described the scene around 1700:

As the slaves come down to Fida [modern Ghana, on the Gold Coast] from the inland country, they are put into a booth or prison . . . near the beach, and when the Europeans are to receive them, they are brought out onto a large plain, where the ship's surgeons examine every part of everyone of them, to the smallest member, men and women being stark naked. . . . Such as are allowed good and sound are set on one side . . . marked on the breast with a red-hot iron, imprinting the mark of the French, English, or Dutch companies. . . . The branded slaves after this are returned to their former booths where they await shipment, sometimes 10–15 days.

Eventually, the buyers made their final selections and herded the slaves aboard the ships. The typical colonial slaver was a 50-ton sailing sloop or schooner. Normally, such ships had a single deck with a deep hold below. But the slavers modified them, adding one or more subdecks at intervals of three feet or less, to accommodate their human cargo. An average such vessel carried a crew of 6 to 10 men and from 100 to 200 slaves.

The torturous 9-to-12 week journey across the Atlantic became known as the "middle passage." Crews packed the slaves tightly into the narrow subdecks with no regard for the slaves' comfort, safety, or sanitation. It was common for the captives to lie in their own or their fellows' excrement. When the stench became so bad that even the crew could no longer stand it, crew members doused the compartments with vinegar. The lack of moving and breathing space was both stifling and terrifying. A doctor, Alexander Falconbridge, who witnessed such conditions on several slave ship voyages, wrote an account in 1788:

The height, sometimes, between decks, was only 18 inches; so that the unfortunate human beings could not turn around, or even on their sides, the elevation being less than the breadth of their shoulders; and here they are usually chained to the decks by the neck and legs. In such a place, the sense of misery and suffocation is so great, that the Negroes . . . are driven to frenzy.

Rescued from a slave ship by an abolitionist sea captain, young Africans await their first food in days. Starvation was only one of the horrors threatening captured blacks on their journey to the New World.

These horrifying conditions were somewhat improved by good weather conditions. On clear, calm days at sea, the crew brought groups of the slaves up onto the main deck and "danced" them, or forced them to jog and hop in place as one of the captives beat time on a drum. The object was to exercise the slaves and keep their muscles in tone. They were, after all, valuable property to be exploited in waiting American markets. The crews also mistakenly believed that dancing the slaves helped reduce the incidence of scurvy, a disease characterized by bleeding gums and extreme weakness, which many slaves contracted during the middle passage. (Scurvy is caused by a deficiency of vitamin C, but this information was not yet generally available.) The act of dancing in heavy leg irons was painful, but it was an improvement over the horrors of life belowdecks.

The worst conditions the slaves encountered during the middle passage were those they endured in poor weather, when the crew kept them belowdecks for as much as a week at a time. In his account Falconbridge reported,

> Some wet and blowing weather having occasioned the port-holes to be shut and the grating [the hatch leading below decks] to be covered, fluxes [diarrhea] and fevers among the Negroes ensued. While they were in this situation, I frequently went down among them till at length their rooms [the slave holds] became so extremely hot as to be only bearable for a very short time. . . . The floor of their rooms, was so covered with the blood and mucus which had proceeded [flowed] from them in consequence of the flux, that it resembled a slaughterhouse. . . . Numbers of the slaves having fainted they were carried upon deck where several of them died and the rest with great difficulty were restored [to a semblance of health].

In light of the suffering slaves experienced during the middle passage, it is not surprising that some felt they could take no more and committed suicide by hurling themselves overboard. Attempting to prevent this, many slave captains rigged nets along the sides of their vessels. Other slaves reacted by refusing to eat, which often prompted their captors to pry open their mouths with special screwlike devices and administer food through funnels. Still other captives became so dispirited that they simply stared into space, a condition the slavers called "fixed melancholy."

The ratio of slaves who survived middle passage to those who died from suicide, disease, or maltreatment varied widely from one voyage to another. On average, however, the death rates are estimated to have been 15 to 20 percent. Throughout most of the 18th century, as many as 60,000 Africans survived the middle passage each year. The death toll en route, then, may have been as high as 15,000 people each year. Ironically, partly because of the spread of disease, death rates for whites aboard slave ships were at least as high as for blacks, a situation John Boles and other slavery chroniclers have called "poetic justice."

Occasionally, voyages of middle passage turned out to be disastrous for both blacks and whites—for blacks in terms of loss of life and for whites in financial terms. Some of the highest death tolls were the result of the slavers' callous lack of regard for the lives of their captives. In 1781, for example, the slave ship *Zong* was running short of food and water. Because his insurance covered death by drowning but not by starvation, the ship's captain ordered 132 slaves thrown overboard. Other disasters were produced by a combination of factors, as in the case of the *St. John,* a Dutch vessel that sailed for the Americas with a full load of slaves in May 1659. According to historian Ulrich Phillips, the ship

beat about the [African] coast in search of provisions but found barely enough for daily consumption. . . . Meanwhile bad food had brought dysentery [a severe infection of the intestines], the surgeon, the cooper [barrelmaker], and a sailor had died, and the slave cargo was daily diminishing. Five weeks of sailing then carried the ship across the Atlantic, where . . . she struck a reef near her destination . . . and was abandoned by her officers and crew. Finally a sloop sent . . . to remove the surviving slaves was captured by a privateer [pirate ship] with them on board. Of the 195 Negroes comprising the cargo . . . from one to five died nearly every day, and . . . at the end of the [voyage] . . . the slave loss had reached 110.

At the conclusion of the middle passage the slave ships docked in Virginia, Maryland, and other American colonies. For the slaves, the ordeal of the voyage had ended, but new terrors and indignities awaited. First, they faced the numbing disorientation and fear of being totally helpless in a strange land where even

the language was alien. Some of the captives were certain their captors would kill and eat them; others had no idea what to expect. Then came the slave auctions. Herded onto public auction blocks, the slaves were exhibited as though they were livestock, prodded and examined by prospective buyers. Once sold, they were taken, still chained, to the plantations where they would work for the rest of their lives.

A slaver, her hold crammed with terrified, underfed blacks, plows across the choppy Atlantic Ocean. "In such a place [as a slave ship]," noted one naval doctor, "the sense of misery and suffocation is so great, that the Negroes . . . are driven to frenzy."

After suffering the trauma of capture, the cruelties of the Atlantic voyage, and the humiliation of being bought, the slaves were now expected to adjust quickly to plantation life. Some simply could not do it, repeatedly trying to escape and suffering torture and death as a result. Others were so weak from the ordeal of the voyage that they contracted and soon died from New World diseases for which they had no immunity. As many as one in three of the slaves who arrived in the colonies died in the first year of captivity. Most newcomers, however, did live and did manage to adjust. But the horror and hopelessness of their predicament remained, a legacy they passed on to their children.

For the most part the slave owners seemed unconcerned about the misery their slaves had thus far endured. From the white point of view slaves were racially and morally inferior beings, making it seem acceptable to treat them like animals. Even the churches supported slavery, regarding the white ownership of blacks as natural. Clergymen of all faiths followed the lead of the Catholic Church, which had endorsed slavery even before the first slaves arrived in Jamestown. In 1610, for example, a high-ranking churchman wrote to a scholar-priest, asking if trading and owning slaves conformed to church doctrine. The priest answered,

> Your Reverence writes me that you would like to know whether the Negroes who are sent to your parts have been legally captured. To this I reply that your reverence should have no scruples [ethical objections] on this point, because this is a matter which has been questioned by the [Church's] Board of conscience . . . and all its members are learned and conscientious men. . . . We have been here ourselves for 40 years and there have been among us very learned fathers. . . . Never did they consider the [slave] trade as illicit [illegal]. Therefore we . . . buy these slaves for our service without any scruple.

With the churches and their leaders condoning and even taking part in slave ownership, few everyday people questioned the morality of slavery or of the trade that made it possible. Thus, with slavery an accepted fact of life, the slave ships continued on their unrelenting voyages of despair.

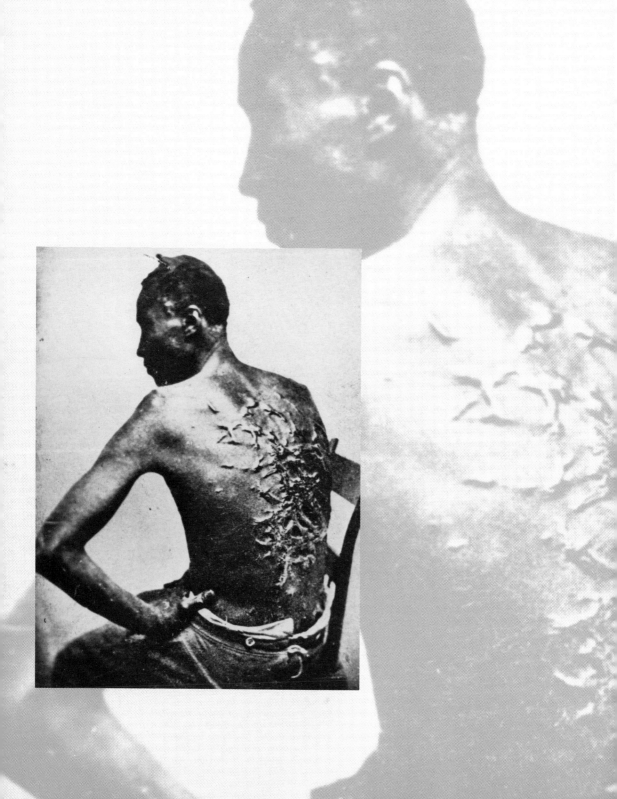

6

MASTER AND SLAVE: MAINTAINING CONTROL

COLONIAL slave owners controlled their captured Africans with threats and force; beatings were freely administered, either as punishments or as examples for other potentially disobedient slaves. As Peter Kolchin has put it, "Born in violence, slavery survived by the lash. . . . The routine functioning of southern farms and plantations rested on the authority of the owners and their representatives, supported by the state, to inflict pain on their human property."

Racism, which had been steadily increasing since the 1600s, gave slaveholders a free hand in employing these harsh methods. Long gone were the days when blacks and whites worked side by side in the fields and slaves could even earn their freedom through hard work. In the 1700s, especially in the southern slave economy, the relationship of master to slave had become strictly that of owner to property. Black skin and ways were no longer just "different"; they were "inferior." Whites' belief in their own racial supe-

A 19th-century photograph gives mute evidence of the savage whipping endured by an enslaved African American. Slave punishments were widespread from the colonial period on, although masters who practiced extraordinary cruelty were in the minority.

riority extended throughout their community, sub-scribed to by slave owners and nonowners alike. As long as white society saw blacks as somehow less than human, their enslavement and any means necessary to enforce it seemed justified. The use of coercion against blacks was necessary: they must be made to do their masters' bidding, and they must be unshakably persuaded of the folly of revolt. Thus racism and force went hand-in-hand, clearly defining the master-slave relationship.

Whites did not have to look far for "proof" of black inferiority. For centuries Europeans had re-garded the very idea of "blackness" as negative, some-thing suggesting evil, malignance, and death. With such an inbuilt prejudice, whites saw Africans not simply as people who happened to have dark skins: God, they assumed, must have made them dark for a reason—to differentiate the bad race from the good, to draw a distinct color line between the natural master and the natural slave.

Christian whites, moreover, considered Africans "heathens"—unbelievers who were less civilized and righteous than themselves. To further justify their attitude, whites quoted the Bible, specifically the book of Genesis, which tells of Noah's youngest son, Ham, fathering the dark races of Africa. When Ham embarrassed him, Noah condemned him to be a slave to his brothers, who went on to father the lighter-skinned races. Colonial slavery supporters interpreted the story as proof that blacks were meant to serve whites.

Whether they owned slaves or not—and most did not—southern whites tacitly supported slavery. Non-owners, for example, could usually be counted on to help recapture their neighbors' runaway slaves. Un-derlying this white solidarity was the knowledge that blacks who remained in servitude posed no economic threat to whites. The majority of the South's white males were small farmers or landless workers who could not afford to own slaves and who had no wish to compete for jobs with free blacks. These "poor whites" approved a system that not only guaranteed them their choice of jobs but allowed them to identify with the white ruling powers.

White fear of slave uprisings was another factor that fueled racism, segregation, and brutal methods of controlling blacks. Slaves comprised a substantial portion of the population—as high as one-third in Maryland in 1750, for example—and posed an ongoing potential threat to their masters. That many slave owners worried about this threat is illustrated by a 1736 entry from the now widely studied *Secret Diary* of William Byrd, a wealthy Virginia planter. Byrd wrote,

> We have already at least 10,000 men of these descendants of Ham, fit to bear arms, and these numbers increase every day, as well by birth as by importation. And in case there should arise a [black] man of desperate fortune, he might . . . kindle a servile [slave] war . . . and tinge our rivers wide as they are with blood.

Occasional slave uprisings did occur, convincing William Byrd and other masters that their worst fears were well-founded. The first large-scale colonial slave revolt took place in 1712 in New York, where about 25 blacks set fire to a building and killed 9 whites. The rebels were quickly caught, tried, and condemned to death. Most were burned or hanged, but one was cooked over a slow fire for 10 hours, serving as a ghastly lesson to other would-be rebels.

Southerners watched these events with concern. If such an incident could happen in New York, where blacks made up only 10 percent of the population, another, they reasoned, could easily happen at home. They were right. In 1720 some South Carolina planters uncovered a slave plot that involved the wholesale killing of whites. Foiling the plan before it could be put into action, the planters burned and hanged the ringleaders.

Another rebellion occurred in 1739 at Stono, a plantation in Saint Paul's Parish, South Carolina (about 20 miles from Charleston). Howard Zinn describes the scene:

> About 20 slaves rebelled, killed two warehouse guards, stole guns and gunpowder, and headed south, killing people in their way, and burning buildings. They were joined by others, until there were perhaps 80 slaves in all and, according to one account of the time, "they called out Liberty, marched on with Colors [flags] displayed, and two Drums beating." The militia found and attacked them. In the ensuing battle, perhaps 50 slaves and 25 whites were killed before the uprising was crushed.

The Stono Rebellion was no isolated incident. Scholar Herbert Aptheker says (in *American Negro Slave Revolts*) that at least 250 rebellions or conspiracies involving 10 or more slaves occurred, most of them during the 1700s. In addition to those slaves who rebelled in this period, thousands ran away from their masters.

The slaveholders' anxiety about keeping their slaves under control was reflected by the laws they passed—harsh statutes that gave whites nearly unlimited latitude in restricting and punishing blacks. A section of Virginia's slave code from the 1700s, for example, contained this passage:

> Whereas many times slaves run away . . . if the slave does not immediately return, anyone whatsoever may kill or destroy such slaves by such ways and means as he . . . shall think fit. . . . If the slave is apprehended . . . it shall . . . be lawful . . . to order such punishment for the said slave, either by dismembering, or in any other way . . . as [masters] in their discretion shall think fit, for the reclaiming any

in their discretion shall think fit, for the reclaiming any such incorrigible slave, and terrifying others from the like practices.

Coercion was the main instrument by which slaves were controlled. They were drilled in specific concepts: to "know their place," be awed by their

Wealthy and cultured, Virginia planter William Byrd regarded himself a civilized man. Nevertheless, in his diary he recalled whipping slaves for minor offenses.

owners' power and that of white society in general, and live only to serve their masters. To make sure they stayed in their "place," owners employed a range of severe punishments. Perhaps the most common was whipping, at the time a standard punishment for lawbreakers of any color.

Minor offenses brought on the lash, but more serious transgressions drew worse: branding with hot irons, slitting the nose, amputating the ears, toes, and fingers (or feet in the case of persistent runaways), extracting teeth, scalding with boiling water, and castration. For the most serious crime, that of killing a white person, the penalty, not surprisingly, was certain death. In 1767 in Virginia, four slaves who had killed their overseer were hanged and their heads cut off and publicly displayed. And in Louisiana in 1780 a black woman who had killed a white girl had her hand cut off before she was hanged. After the execution, officials nailed the woman's head and hand to a post in the center of town.

Not all slave owners, of course, treated their human property with cruelty. Many took pride in what they regarded as fair and humane treatment of their slaves, feeding them well and seeing that they received competent medical attention. Some masters demonstrated a fatherly attitude toward their workers: referring to his black workers in a 1740 diary entry, William Byrd says, "I talked with my people." And such affection was often returned, for example by the many black "mammies" who demonstrated genuine love for the white children they raised for their masters.

Even paternalistic slaveholders, however, inflicted punishments on their workers. William Byrd's diary is filled with entries describing the whipping of black servants for a wide variety of relatively minor offenses, such as "stealing the rum and filling the bottle up with water." Sometimes he chastised slaves

simply to vent his own frustrations. An October 1710 diary entry reads: "I went to my lodgings but my man [personal servant] was gone to bed and I was shut out. However I called him and beat him for it."

Despite such incidents, Byrd considered himself a lenient master, especially in contrast with his wife, whom he often reprimanded for her violence toward

Plantation workers enjoy an uncommon free afternoon. As the black population increased, African American traditions and culture established ever-deepening roots in the slave community.

Two white girls (far right) sneak onto a happy scene in the slave quarters. Entitled "Old Kentucky Home," this 19th-century painting offers a highly romanticized view of plantation life.

the family's slaves. On July 15, 1710, for example, he wrote, "My wife against my will caused little Jenny [a young slave] to be burned with a hot iron, for which I quarreled with her." And on March 2, 1712, Byrd wrote, "I had a terrible quarrel with my wife concerning Jenny that I took away from her when she was beating her with the [fireplace] tongs."

But while masters used strict methods to keep their slaves obedient, few much cared what they did on their own time and in their own quarters. This lack of

interest allowed African Americans to develop their own sense of community and identity. Endless labor and discipline may sometimes have broken their bodies, but nothing broke their spirits. All through the 18th century those spirits would create a new and unique culture amid, but distinctly separate from, the white society that imprisoned them.

7

THE GROWTH OF AFRICAN AMERICAN CULTURE

THE culture that Africans developed in America was neither African nor American. Containing elements from both sources, it was a new and unique hybrid, forged in the bleak conditions of servitude. This new culture gave the slaves a feeling of community and also allowed them, after being torn away from their roots, to find a sense of identity as a people. The customs, beliefs, attitudes, and modes of expression that blacks shaped in the 18th century became part of a rich cultural heritage that helped form the black American character.

Ironically, part of the new cultural identity that developed among American slaves—a sense of "Africanness"—had never existed in Africa. As historian John Boles points out,

> Slaves came from a wide geographical swath of Africa, spoke different tongues, carried with them a variety of customs and beliefs, and did not even conceive of themselves as Africans; instead, they identified themselves by tribe or clan, considering other black peoples no more related to them than contemporary Englishmen felt re-

Followed by bloodhounds (on far bank of water), terrified runaways make their way through a trackless southern swamp. The farther removed from Africa that blacks became, the more likely they were to try to escape alone rather than in a group.

lated to Italians. There was no one African culture. When
an African chieftain sold to waiting slavers blacks captured from an enemy, he was not selling his "brothers."

Out of their common bondage in America, blacks
of differing African heritages came to feel a kind of
brotherhood. Each black individual—or his parents
or grandparents—had come from the same faraway
continent and experienced the same terrifying proce-
dures of capture, transport, and sale. In addition to
their family backgrounds, American blacks shared
some cultural traits and practices that linked nearly
all the tribes and kingdoms of western and central
Africa.

Among these common points was the perception
of time, which in Africa was quite different from its
European counterpart. Rather than thinking in such
units as years and centuries, Africans thought in terms
of cycles, such as the duration of generations or ruling
dynasties; because their vision of time was so vast,
Africans tended to have more patience than Europeans. Also common to most Africans was their un-
derstanding of land ownership. To a European, land
was measurable, a solid entity that could be owned and
passed down within a family. To an African, on the
other hand, borders were vague and the concept of
land more spiritual than practical; if land "belonged"
to anyone, it belonged to an entire tribe or kingdom,
or to the gods. Family relationships, including the
acceptance of polygamous marriages, tended to be
similar across western Africa, as did such religious
concepts as ancestor worship and belief in magic,
nature gods, and spirits.

When they first arrived in America, the captive
Africans must have viewed colonial society with both
horror and wonder. Everything they saw and heard—
language, food, transportation, clothing—would have
been strange and frightening. At first, newly arrived
Africans held fast to their old beliefs and ways, but in

time most realized that the only way to survive was to live as their captors did, shedding a large measure of their ancestral ideas and ways. And as the enslaved Africans produced children—who never had and never would experience Africa—their culture receded still further. As American-born blacks began to outnumber African-born blacks, Africa must have seemed more remote than ever.

Illustrating this Americanization process was the change in infant-feeding practices. Only in areas of the New World where large numbers of blacks lived in close proximity and had minimal contact with white society, such as the Caribbean sugarcane plantations, did black women continue to nurse their babies for extended periods. In the North American colonies slaves lived in smaller, more scattered groups and had constant exposure to white society and its ways. Blacks in these areas adopted the shorter breast-feeding period of Europeans relatively quickly.

The evolution of slave flight is another example of Americanizing. The goals and methods of runaway slaves changed markedly from African-born to American-born generations. Peter Kolchin writes,

> In both the upper and lower South, newly enslaved Africans often fled in groups, striving somehow either to return to Africa or to establish African-style villages on the frontier. [American-born] fugitives, by contrast, showed less interest in replicating African communal culture than in avoiding detection, and therefore usually absconded alone. . . . Flight continued to be a pervasive feature of slavery, but runaway slaves adjusted their tactics to local conditions so as to maximize their chances of success.

Also illustrating the transformation from African to African American culture was the process of naming children. Although some masters provided names for their newly born slaves, by the mid-1700s most blacks were allowed to name their own offspring. At this point, distinct patterns of naming emerged; the use of purely African names decreased, and the num-

A slave trader (center) gestures toward a woman he has just sold as she reaches desperately for her child, now the property of another slaveholder. Separation of families was among slavery's cruelest features.

ber of European names increased. Biblical names became especially popular with blacks. According to one study of slaves in the Carolinas, Old Testament names increased to 10 percent of the total by 1750 and 20 percent by 1800. Another change involved the meanings of names. In Africa many names came from the days of the week; a child born on a Friday, for example, might be named for that day: "Cuffee." In time this meaning was lost, and a Cuffee would be just as likely to have been born on a Monday as on a Friday.

At the same time, the American-born slave population retained some traditional naming patterns, giving their emerging culture a uniquely African flavor. For example, in Africa a person's surname often indicated his or her place of birth, important because such locations were associated with highly esteemed ancestors. This custom carried over to African American culture; even when slaves were sold, they tended to identify themselves with their original owner, or even their parents' or grandparents' owner. For example, Nat Turner, the slave who led a famous revolt in 1831, belonged to Joseph Travis, but he retained the surname of Benjamin Turner, owner of the farm where he had been born. In this way American slaves held onto an African custom that continued to link them to their ancestral birthplaces.

Another element of the transition from African to African American culture was the black American family. During the colonial period, elaborate kinship and friendship systems emerged in the slave population. At first, slaves from different parts of Africa felt little bond with one another. In time, however, slaves began to intermarry from one plantation to another, in the process forming extended families that grew spatially, or outward from specific geographic locations. John Boles explains,

> By the middle of the 18th century persons identified themselves in relation to quite extended kinship networks that were often actually genealogical: grandparents, parents, siblings, aunts and uncles, nephews, first and second and third cousins. When families were broken up, husbands and teenage children would typically be sold to nearby planters; at a master's death slaves were often willed to elder sons and moved to new locations—usually only a few miles away in the 18th century. By this process kinship and friendship networks expanded spatially. A young child sold away to another plantation might find there an uncle, or an elder sibling, or a relative of a friend on his prior plantation.

Although the formation of large extended families within a small geographic region was a common aspect of colonial African American culture, not all families were lucky enough to maintain such close contact among members. In every colony there were instances of owners selling slaves to other owners living far away. In most such cases, the sold slave never saw his or her family members again. One of the cruelest examples of this practice was the selling of children. According to historian Lorenzo Johnston Greene in his book *The Negro in Colonial New England,*

Offspring of slaves became the property of the woman's owner and as such were economic assets in the possession of the master. They were sometimes taken from their parents and sold with as little restraint as one would sell a calf, pig, or colt. . . . In one instance even an infant was sold when in 1738, Ezekiel Chase of Newbury, Massachusetts, sold to John Merrill for forty pounds, his "Negro boy Titus about one year and a half old."

Disrupted black families had little or no chance of reuniting with their lost loved ones, but they sometimes tried anyway. In 1773, a group of Boston blacks petitioned the Massachusetts legislature for their freedom and an end to the breakup of families. Their plea, which had no effect, said in part,

Our children are . . . taken from us by force and sent miles from us [where] we seldom or ever see them again there to be made slaves of for Life which sometimes is [very] short by Reason of Being dragged from their mothers [breast].

Another factor in the creation of the new African American community was common language. Slaves fresh from Africa spoke many different tongues. That, combined with their unfamiliarity with English, surely added to the confusion and misery of the enslavement process. Over the course of their first year or so in America, however, new slaves learned a pidgin, or mixed, language composed of both African and English words and phrases. Gradually becoming more complex, this patois spread throughout the colonies, becoming a cultural link among blacks and helping to shape the unique character of the emerging African American community. "Breaking the language barrier was an inspiring accomplishment," comments John Boles, "for it allowed bonds of friendship and shared emotions to start wearing away the alienation, even disorientation, and begin creating the matrix [core] of black solidarity."

The fictional slave Uncle Remus entertains "young massa" with another of his funny, inventive, African-based tales about animals whose behavior is all too human.

Africans in America quickly adapted to white social customs and language, but religion was another matter. For more than a century after the 1619 arrival of the first Africans, most New World blacks practiced the religion of their home countries. A type of animism, this faith generally stressed the relationship of the worshipers with their ancestors as well as with various nature gods and spirits and a more remote and largely unknowable High God who ruled over all.

Many slaves held on to African rituals as a way of keeping their connection to Africa alive. Other factors, too, accounted for these practices' long survival in the New World. First, many masters were indifferent about their slaves' spiritual lives: as long as they did it quietly and in whatever free time they had, slaves could worship as they wished. Indirectly, some owners actually encouraged the continuance of African religious beliefs: because they feared that the Christian message—all souls are equal before God—would give slaves dangerous ideas, they forbade the teaching of Christianity to blacks.

American slaves held onto their traditional beliefs until the mid-1700s, when some Christian ministers began preaching to blacks. Most slaves, especially the older generations, rejected Christian ideas at first. Their general feelings were perhaps reflected in the words of an African-born, American-raised slave around 1730. Invited to listen to a Maryland clergyman speak, he declined politely. "The religion of this country," he said, "[is] altogether false, and indeed, no religion at all."

Nevertheless, during the "Great Awakening"—a revival of religious fervor that swept America in the 1730s and 1740s—Christianity did enroll thousands of blacks, most of them born in America and thus less connected with the old African beliefs. The willingness of some Protestant churches, notably the Baptists and Methodists, to welcome the downtrodden, even nonwhites, made these denominations especially popular with blacks. In the 1770s and 1780s a fresh Christian revival swept through the land. No reliable figures exist for the number of black Christians at the time, but the increasing importance of Christianity among blacks is demonstrated by the appearance of the first black Christian churches: one opened in

Brer Rabbit matches wits with Brer Fox in a typical Uncle Remus story. These characters and their antics were widely popularized by 19th-century white author Joel C. Harris, but they had originated in the slave community many decades earlier.

South Carolina in 1773; another in Virginia three years later. Historian Kolchin observes,

> The Christianization of American blacks was an uneven process: it proceeded in fits and starts, was welcomed by some . . . more readily than others, and generally progressed least rapidly in areas of heavy black concentration such as the South Carolina and Georgia low country. Still, over the course of the 18th century, an increasing proportion of slaves were exposed to—and embraced—the religion of their masters.

Other important aspects of the emerging African American culture were music and oral literature. Both had been key elements of most West African cultures, and their Americanized versions flowered in the 18th

Slaves celebrate the end of corn-shucking season by singing traditional spirituals. Blending elements from West Africa, Europe, and the New World, African Americans developed their own highly original music, ranging from hymns and dirges to work songs, marches, and jazz.

century. In his book, *These United States: The Questions of Our Past*, historian Irwin Unger states,

> Slaves sang about God and salvation, about their work, about love and passion, and about their daily lives. They composed humorous songs, bitter songs, and even rebellious songs that explicitly called for freedom. They also composed stories and poems. Talented black storytellers drew on the west African tradition of oral history, fable, and legend, combined it with Bible tales, and filled their stories with the animals and people of the southern environment. . . . One of the best-known groups of tales concerns Brer Rabbit, who manages to outwit stronger animals with his resourcefulness and his trickery.

Songs and oral literature flourished in the slave quarters; there, after the day's work ended, blacks expressed themselves in ways distinct from those of their masters. Their personal activities frequently belied the fact that they were human property. "When the master's work was done," comments Kolchin, "[the slaves] ate, sang, prayed, played, talked, quarreled, made love, hunted, fished, named babies, cleaned house . . . and rested. . . . Christmas, harvest time, corn shucking, and hog killing provided occasions for celebrations that slaves eagerly anticipated and long remembered." As black historian Lerone Bennett, Jr., explains in his book *Before the Mayflower: A History of Black America*,

> On most plantations, there were two parties: "the dancing party" and "the praying party." . . . On holidays, especially at Christmas, the slaves kicked up their heels in joyous dances, drank strong liquor and persimmon beer, and sang "devil songs.". . . Saturday night was the dancing party's night. In barns and open fields and in slave-row shacks, slaves did jigs, shuffles, and "set de flo." They danced to the fiddle or the banjo and beat out rhythms with sticks and bones or by clapping their hands and stomping their feet. The slaves had a word for it even then. A "cool cat" in those days was a "ring-clipper." . . . The praying party held forth on Sundays. . . . Out of these . . . meetings and the wakes [funerals] and other mournful events of the slave quarters came the Negro spirituals.

A spiritual might express joy—"I went down in the valley to pray/My soul got happy and I stayed all day"; optimism—"I looked over Jordan and what did I see?/A band of angels comin' after me,/Comin' for to carry me home"; or deep religious faith—"A little talk with Jesus makes it right," "I know the Lord's laid his hands on

Shielding their campfire's light with a wooden lean-to, fugitive slaves spend the night in a Louisiana bayou. From the beginning of American black slavery, escape was uppermost in the minds of many blacks.

me," "O, my good Lord, show me the way." A great proportion of the spirituals, however, express grief over life's sorrows; the slaves sang of the weight of their chains, their forced separation from the people they loved, and their eternal weariness.

> I'll lie in de grave and stretch out my arms;
> Lay dis body down.
> I go to de judgment in de evenin' of de day,
> When I lay dis body down;

> And my soul and your soul will meet in de day
> When I lay dis body down.

One white observer, Thomas Wentworth Higginson, found himself tremendously moved when he heard a group of blacks singing "Lay Dis Body Down." "Never, it seems to me," he said, "since man first lived and suffered, was his infinite longing for peace uttered more plaintively."

Black music, asserts historian Bennett, "went back to the slave cabins and further, back to the polyrhythmic complexity of the forgotten land—West Africa. The music was a melding of African, European, and American elements, [and consisted] of spirituals and work songs; of cries and hollers; of 'devil songs' and shouts and stomps; of slow drags, marches, funeral dirges, and hymns. It was a blend and yet it was new. A thing made in America by illiterate and despised Negroes."

As African American culture emerged, the slaves also developed their own work routines and displayed the ability to perform a wide variety of jobs well. The great diversity of slave occupations had a profound effect, not only on black culture but on white southern society.

8

THE LONG ROAD

THE traditional view of black slaves serving mainly as field hands and unskilled laborers—an image often portrayed in modern novels and movies—is misleading. In the colonial period, slaves served in a surprisingly wide range of jobs in both the South and the North. The growth of a larger array of slave occupations, some of them carrying serious responsibilities, afforded at least a few blacks the chance for upward mobility—rare in a society that considered dark-skinned people barely human.

By the mid-18th century, the South had become heavily dependent on its slaves, who filled a wide variety of the area's jobs. Historian Lorenzo Greene notes that in slaveholders' homes,

> Negro women served as cooks, laundresses, maids, nurses, and as general household workers, but they were also trained in domestic arts [such as] spinning, knitting and weaving. . . . The male slaves not only performed the heavy work about the house but also acted as cooks, coachmen, attendants, butlers, and valets. The employment of Negro

Crispus Attucks, the first casualty in America's fight for independence, falls to a British musket ball during the Boston Massacre of March 5, 1770. A self-educated escaped slave, Attucks had been discussing unfair British taxation with other Boston patriots just before his fatal encounter with the redcoats.

men in such capacities is indicated by contemporary news-
papers. One paper lists [an advertisement for] a boy "who
can speak French" and is "very fit for a valet," another cites
a Negro who is "a very good cook."

Along with domestic and field labor, plantation
slaves fished and hunted to bring food for their master's table; they also served as their estates' carpenters,
coopers, and blacksmiths. There had been precedents
for many of these jobs in western Africa; Africans
routinely hunted, fished, raised livestock, and con-
structed relatively complex homes and villages, all of
which meant that many African-born slaves required
little extensive training in farm-oriented occupations.
Readily adapting themselves to such jobs, they also
trained their children to do them.

Slaves rapidly developed their own work routines.
To the rhythm of songs, many of them based on
African music, field workers moved through rows of
crops, swinging their tools in measured strokes. Carpenters, blacksmiths, and others also created work
patterns that made their jobs easier. Slaves, then, were
not simply robotic laborers, dependent on white overseers for training and guidance. Most slaves, despite
the indignity of servitude, took the initiative and
helped develop the most productive and energy-
efficient ways of doing their jobs. "Africans were not
simply what the white man made them," writes John
Boles. "To an extent only recently realized, Africans
had a hand in shaping what and who they became in
America."

Many slaves performed their jobs so well that their
owners relied on them completely, assigning them
ever more responsible and skilled positions. On farms
and plantations, workers included the millers who
ground grain into flour, horse breeders and gardeners,
butlers who oversaw the entire household, and "mammies" who helped raise their owners' children. On
large estates a trusted, extremely competent slave

might become a driver, which involved the supervision and discipline of other blacks. Historian Lerone Bennett, Jr., quotes one planter who said, "The head driver . . . is not required to work like other hands. He is to be treated with more respect than any other Negro by both master and overseer [plantation manager]." The driver, whose interests lay with the master and the feared and hated overseer, was—not surprisingly—usually despised by his fellow slaves.

Slaves also held important positions in non-agri-

After delivering his master to church, a Virginia coachman waits outside with a friend. By the mid-1700s blacks had mastered almost as wide a variety of jobs as whites, in the process becoming indispensable in the colonies' day-to-day life.

cultural areas. In such southern cities as Charleston, South Carolina, and Richmond, Virginia, white businessmen employed slaves, although usually only as errand boys, porters, ditch diggers, and the like. Even in the South, however, some slaves worked themselves into more skilled professions, serving as ship builders, lumber mill operators, iron forgers, rope makers, carpenters, tanners, and printers' assistants. There were also black bakers, tailors, and distillers of alcohol. In northern cities slaves worked in skilled trades and performed a wide variety of mercantile and industrial tasks. And in New England a few blacks attained the highly respectable position of doctor's apprentice.

Jobs at that level, however, were few. Hobbled by racial intolerance, limited education, and lack of training, blacks achieved little professional or financial success, even in the relatively liberal North. Nevertheless, some members of the African American community managed to build spectacular careers. Among these gifted men was Paul Cuffe.

Born on Cuttyhunk Island, Massachusetts, in 1759, Paul Cuffe was the son of a West African–born former slave father and a Wampanoag Indian mother. Cuffe went to sea when he was 14. Proving himself a quick learner, he soon gained the respect of the maritime community in the Northeast's ports. By the time he reached the age of 25 he was master of his own ship—a small, open boat of less than 10 tons—and on the way to being a rich man. He soon bought the *Ranger,* the *Traveller,* and the *Alpha,* large merchant ships with which he made impressive profits in the coastal trade.

Cuffe invested well; his fortune in land and homes was among the largest in the colony.

Paul Cuffe, seen in silhouette in this 1812 engraving, would have been a remarkable man in any era. Born free in 1759, he went to sea at the age of 14, then acquired a fleet of merchant ships, became rich and famous, crusaded for the abolition of slavery and black civil rights, and worked toward building a new African nation of former American slaves.

When Congress levied stiff taxes to finance the American Revolution, which began in 1775, the wealthy Cuffe was told he owed a vast amount of money; he astonished officials by refusing to pay. As long as he and other blacks were denied the right to vote, said Cuffe, he would deny the government the right to collect his taxes as an American citizen. By the end of the Revolution in 1783, Massachusetts would take the unusual step of granting the vote to all free black adult males. (No American women of any color would gain that privilege for almost 150 years.) In later years Cuffe was to become a leader of the colonization movement, which aimed at ending slavery by sending America's black population to colonize Africa or Central America.

In agriculture, industry, and the trades, the number of skilled slaves and free blacks increased over the course of the colonial period. A 1710 census of four Maryland counties, for example, shows 4 out of the 525 male slaves as skilled workers. Just a decade later, the number of skilled male slaves in the same counties had risen to 13 out of 213. Shortly after the end of the colonial period, the ratio of skilled to unskilled slaves in all of the colonies was higher still. In 1786 George Washington had 41 adult slaves on his Virginia plantation; among them were four carpenters, four spinners, three drivers and stablers, two blacksmiths, two seamstresses, a wagon maker, a gardener, and several cooks.

George Mason, son of a wealthy Virginia planter, wrote about the slaves on his family's estate in the 1770s; his recollections illustrate the broad diversity of slave occupations and the degree to which skilled slaves supported colonial plantation life.

It was very much the practice with gentlemen of landed and slave estates in the interior of Virginia, so to organize them as to have considerable resources within themselves. . . . [My father's] carpenters and sawyers built and kept in repair all the dwelling-houses, barns, stables, ploughs, harrows [large plowing devices], gates, etc., on the plantations and the outhouses at the home house. His coopers made the hogsheads [large casks] the tobacco was prized in and the tight casks to hold the cider and other liquors. The tanners and curriers with the proper vats etc., tanned and dressed the skins well . . . and shoemakers made them into shoes for the negroes. . . . The blacksmith did all the iron work required by the establishment, as making and repairing ploughs, harrows, teeth chains, bolts, etc., etc. The spinners, weavers and knitters made all the coarse cloths and stockings used by the negroes, and some of the finer texture worn by the white family, nearly all [the clothes] worn by the children of it. . . . All these operations were carried on at the home house, and their results distributed as occasion required to the different plantations.

In the North the need for slave labor had been minimal even in the 1600s, mainly because of the absence of large-scale plantation agriculture. Because business and industry tended to employ cheap white labor, the demand for slaves in the North steadily decreased. In 1715 the New England colonies had only about 4,150 slaves out of a total population of some 158,000, or about 1 black for every 39 whites. By the end of the colonial period the ratio of blacks to whites in New England was 1 in 60 and steadily dropping. Even in New York State, which had the largest number of slaves and slave owners of any northern colony during the 18th century, only 1 in 5 whites owned slaves.

At the time, religion, like other social institutions, did not question the principle of one person owning another. Not until the 1760s, near the end of the colonial period, did one sect, the Quakers, start to label slavery morally wrong. Yet religious New Englanders, slave owners included, believed that slaves had souls. They also believed that a person could save his or her soul only through firsthand knowledge of the Bible. The laws of most southern colonies forbade anyone to teach a slave to read, but in the North, as Lorenzo Greene explains,

> Many masters . . . gave their slaves instruction in reading, writing, and the trades. Members of the Congregational clergy . . . also pioneered in the secular instruction of the slaves. Performing a similar service were such organizations as the Quakers, the Society for the Propagation of the Gospel, and the Associates of Dr. Bray. The two latter organizations, which were connected with the Anglican church, not only provided missionaries, books, Bibles, and

Phillis Wheatley is pictured at her writing desk in this engraving, published in 1773 as the frontispiece of her first and only poetry collection, Poems on Various Subjects, Religious and Moral. *America's first black female poet, Wheatley was the property of a Boston family until they freed her, at the age of 19, in 1773.*

other materials for the Negroes, but also opened schools for them. . . . Many Negroes, like Newport Gardner [musician and teacher], Lemuel Haynes [farm manager and Revolutionary War soldier], and Lucy Terry [poet], by virtue of such instruction, became useful members of their communities, while Phillis Wheatley, the poetess, achieved international fame.

Phillis Wheatley, America's first black female poet, was born about 1754, probably in what is now Gambia in West Africa. Enslaved and brought to America at the age of eight, she was bought by Susannah Wheatley, the wife of a wealthy Boston merchant. Wheatley gave her a new name—"Phillis" after the slave ship that delivered her, and "Wheatley" for her new owners—taught her to speak and read English, and introduced her to the Bible. Realizing that the young slave was unusually bright, the Wheatleys encouraged her to study literature and Latin.

Phillis, who was better educated than many whites of the time, began writing poetry when she was 14. With the help of the Wheatleys and their friends she published *Poems on Various Subjects, Religious and Moral* in 1773, garnering high praise from readers in both America and England. Soon after the book appeared, the Wheatleys granted the poet her freedom. In 1775 she sent George Washington a poetic tribute she had written for him. The revolutionary war general responded by praising her talents and inviting her to visit him at his Cambridge, Massachusetts, military headquarters, which she did in 1776. Poor, alone, and forgotten by a once-admiring public, Wheatley died in 1784 at the age of 30.

Phillis Wheatley's work has been praised for its originality and boldness. Her criticisms of slavery and oppression were unusual for her time, especially as she was herself a slave in a society that practiced slavery. That she managed to publish and receive praise for works with such themes suggests the profound difference between northern and southern attitudes toward slavery.

Even more revealing of the difference between northern and southern attitudes toward blacks is the incidence of northern masters freeing their slaves. This practice became increasingly common toward the end of the colonial period. No reliable records exist for the number of free blacks in the North at that time, but scholarly estimates range from 10,000 to 20,000. Life was not easy for such blacks. Their social status was still inferior to that of whites. And economic opportunities for free blacks were far fewer than they were for whites.

Yet a number of former slaves worked hard, saved their money, and managed to establish successful businesses of their own. Few were as financially successful as the commercial shipper Paul Cuffe, but several made names for themselves. Benjamin Banneker, for example, who was born free in Endicott, Maryland, in 1731, became a noted astronomer, mathematician, surveyor (in 1770, he assisted in charting the site of present-day Washington, D.C.), publisher, writer, and leading American intellectual.

In a celebrated exchange of letters with U.S. secretary of state Thomas Jefferson (later the nation's third president), Banneker ably attacked slavery, an argument that earned him strong respect from Jefferson and other eminent whites. From 1791 to 1802, he published an annual almanac for farmers, the first scientific work published by an African American. In

Benjamin Banneker (center) explains his plans for laying out the new federal capital, Washington, D.C., in 1770. An astronomer, mathematician, surveyor, publisher, and writer, Banneker became the first African American to publish a scientific work—a farmer's almanac, which appeared in 1791.

his introductory issue, Banneker noted that it was the work of "a sable [black] Descendant of Africa, who [offers a] demonstration that mental Powers and Endowments are not the exclusive Excellence of white People." The "Rays of Science," he continued, can enlighten people from all countries, "however they may differ in the Colour of their Skin." Banneker also published a scientific study of bees, and made the first accurate computation of the cycle of the 17-year locust, a contribution of great importance to American agriculture. Regarded by countless Americans as a national hero, Banneker's spirit lives on, both through his landmark achievements and as the namesake of numerous present-day American schools.

Jim Riggs, a Massachusetts basket maker, was another black success story. Riggs earned a reputation for fine craftsmanship and received the patronage of some of the most well-to-do white families in the region. And Newport Gardner, the nation's first important black music teacher, built an enviable reputation for his "very numerously attended singing school" in Rhode Island, attracting white as well as black students.

Other free blacks gained recognition by taking part in the revolutionary war. Black patriots in Boston and other cities took part in some of the angry protests against the presence of British troops in those cities. In the notorious Boston Massacre of March 5, 1770, in which British soldiers fired into a small crowd of Bostonians, one of the heroes of the day was Crispus Attucks, a black man.

Because of his role in the Boston Massacre, Attucks remains one of the best-known American blacks of the colonial period. According to historian Bennett:

He was a native of Framingham, Massachusetts, where he was born sometime around 1723. A black man with some Indian blood, Attucks had spent several years as a slave and had escaped. After his escape in 1750, he went to sea as a sailor. Tall, brawny, with a look that "was enough to terrify any person," Attucks was well known around the docks in lower Boston. Attucks was . . . a drifter of sorts, a man who loved freedom and knew what it was worth. He was about 47, fearless and commanding. When he spoke, men listened. When he commanded, men acted.

It was largely Attucks's commanding personality that led to that fateful encounter in Boston. It was he who urged the colonists to stand their ground against a group of "lobsterbacks"—as contemptuous colonists dubbed the red-uniformed British soldiers. The soldiers brandished their bayonets at civilians on King Street, jeers and insults flew, a redcoat clubbed a small Boston boy with his musket, rocks and sticks sailed through the air. Then the soldiers circled defensively

Peter Salem (left, aiming musket) mortally wounds British major John Pitcairn at the 1775 Battle of Bunker Hill. Like many of the 5,000 African Americans who fought in the American Revolution, Salem had won his freedom from slavery by enlisting in the rebel army.

near the custom house, and the crowd closed in. "They dare not fire!" shouted the Bostonians, some of them defiantly adding, "Fire, and be damned!" A flying stick from the crowd struck one of the British soldiers; he fired blindly, instantly killing Attucks. Before the bloody afternoon ended, five Americans lay dead in the snow and the nation was on the road to war.

More than a century later, the city of Boston erected a handsome memorial to the heroes of that day. Accompanying a bronze picture of the scene is a poem, its lines including these:

> And honor to Crispus Attucks, who was leader and voice that day:
> The first to defy, and the first to die . . .

Thus it was that a black man and former slave led the way toward the American fight for freedom.

Of the estimated 30,000 Americans who fought in the revolutionary war, about 5,000 were black. They served for the most part in what would today be called integrated units, fighting the enemy alongside white troops. Dozens of blacks, among them Lemuel Hayes, Samuel Craft, Peter Salem, Caesar Brown, Barzillai Lew, Cato Tufts, and Grant Cooper, fought in every major battle of the war, from Lexington Green and Concord Bridge to Bunker Hill, Trenton, Savannah, and Yorktown, the war's last great engagement. Although at first only free blacks were permitted to enlist in the Continental army, as the war ground on white commanders welcomed all able-bodied volunteers, white and black, slave and free.

Crowding the annals of the revolutionary war are accounts of extraordinary heroism performed by black soldiers. According to an official report, the Negro regiment "distinguished itself by deeds of desperate valor" at the Battle of Rhode Island in 1778; after the Battle of Points Bridge, New York, in 1781, a white officer called the blacks "brave, hardy troops" who "helped gain our liberty and independence." Even the enemy recognized the fighting power and courage of the revolution's black soldiers. "No [American] regiment is to be seen," said one British officer, "in which there are not Negroes in abundance: and among them are able-bodied, strong, and brave fellows."

Black recruitment escalated steadily during the war. "Indeed," says historian John Hope Franklin, "it appeared as though states were now vying with each other in enlisting Negroes." Most states offered freedom to any slave who volunteered to serve for three years; in some cases the government gave slaveholders a land bounty for the blacks they released into the army.

Among the war's outstanding soldiers was Prince Hall, a young black Methodist minister who had been born on the Caribbean island of

Standing at ease, a black revolutionary war soldier displays his full military outfit, from sword and bayonet-tipped musket to backpack and cockaded hat. Blacks from all over the country volunteered to fight for independence; eventually, some 5,000 African Americans served in the war, many with great distinction.

Barbados in 1748 and emigrated to the American colonies in 1765. Hall fought in several revolutionary war battles, including Bunker Hill, at which he was commended for bravery. After the war he was to go on to other battles, fighting for the abolition of slavery, working for schools for black children, and struggling to establish a black branch of the Freemasons, an international benevolent and fraternal order. Hall had been initiated into the Masonic order by a British army lodge of Freemasons in March 1775, but when he asked the American Masonic authorities for permission to start a chapter of black Masons, they refused. In 1784 he applied to the Grand Lodge of England for a charter which was promptly granted. Under that charter, Hall organized African Lodge No. 459, the first black Masonic body in America. Thanks largely to his efforts, black Masonry spread quickly across the young United States.

Fired by the egalitarian sentiments in the Declaration of Independence, some slaveholders freed their bondspeople after America defeated England in 1783. Maryland's Philip Graham, for example, liberated his slaves in 1787, asserting that the keeping of his "fellow men in bondage and slavery is repugnant to the golden law of God and the unalienable right of mankind as well as to every principle of the late glorious revolution which has taken place in America."

But Graham and those who thought as he did were exceptions. Most slaveholders expressed hostility even to the idea of abolishing slavery. A move to condemn slavery in the Declaration of Independence had been quickly stopped, largely to appease slave-owning southerners. That debate marked only the beginning of a rift between North and South; in some ways, the seeds of the Civil War (1861–65), which almost destroyed the young United States, were planted at its birth. After the end of the revolutionary war, the United States would grow and prosper for the next eight decades, but the agent of its near-destruction would not remain buried.

Abraham Lincoln saw the danger clearly. Speaking of his country in 1855, Lincoln said, "Our progress in degeneracy appears to me to be pretty rapid. As a nation we began by declaring that 'all men are created equal.' We now practically read it 'all men are created

Inspecting his Virginia plantation, Mount Vernon, first U.S. president George Washington listens to a black overseer's report. Washington, who owned 300 slaves (many of them inherited), grew increasingly repelled by bondage—"Nothing but the rooting out of slavery," he said, "can perpetuate the existence of our union"—and eventually provided freedom for all his human "property."

equal, except Negroes.'" Two years later, Lincoln—by now speaking for millions of other Americans, both black and white—made his point even clearer. "A house divided against itself cannot stand," he said. "I believe that this nation cannot endure permanently half slave and half free." Despite the warnings of Lincoln and the mighty efforts of courageous men and women of both races, America's blacks were to endure almost 250 years of bondage before emerging into the sunlight of freedom. The road leading to that goal would be long and dark. But it was to be illuminated by qualities that mark the greatest strengths of the human race. Throwing light from surprising, sometimes impossible points along the way were awesome acts of bravery, grace under pressure, intelligence, and desperately hard work. But the strongest light of all came from a people's gallant spirit, a glowing human beacon that stubbornly refused to be extinguished.

FURTHER READING

Bennett, Lerone, Jr. *Before the Mayflower: A History of the Negro in America: 1619–1964*. Baltimore: Penguin Books, 1964.

Boles, John B. *Black Southerners: 1619–1869*. Lexington: University Press of Kentucky, 1984.

Du Bois, W. E. B. *The Suppression of the African Slave Trade to the United States of America: 1639–1870*. New York: Schocken Books, 1969.

Franklin, John Hope. *From Slavery to Freedom: A History of Negro Americans*. New York: Knopf, 1980.

Genovese, Eugene D. *Roll, Jordan, Roll: The World the Slaves Made*. New York: Pantheon Books, 1974.

Gutman, Herbert G. *The Black Family in Slavery and Freedom, 1750–1925*. New York: Pantheon Books, 1976.

July, Robert W. *A History of the African People*. New York: Scribners, 1970.

Kolchin, Peter. *American Slavery: 1619–1877*. New York: Hill and Wang, 1993.

Redding, J. Saunders. *They Came in Chains*. Philadelphia: Lippincott, 1973.

Stampp, Kenneth M. *The Peculiar Institution: Slavery in the Ante-Bellum South*. New York: Knopf, 1963.

INDEX

PICTURE CREDITS

DON NARDO, an award-winning author, has written nearly 50 books, including *The Irish Potato Famine*, *The Mexican-American War*, and *The U.S. Congress*, as well as biographies of Charles Darwin, Thomas Jefferson, and Cleopatra. He lives on Cape Cod, Massachusetts.

CLAYBORNE CARSON, senior consulting editor of the MILESTONES IN BLACK AMERICAN HISTORY series, is a professor of history at Stanford University. His first book, *In Struggle: SNCC and the Black Awakening of the 1960s* (1981), won the Frederick Jackson Turner Prize of the Organization of American Historians. He is the director of the Martin Luther King, Jr., Papers Project, which will publish 12 volumes of King's writings.

DARLENE CLARK HINE, senior consulting editor of the MILESTONES IN BLACK AMERICAN HISTORY series, is the John A. Hannah Professor of American History at Michigan State University. She is the author of numerous books and articles on black women's history. Her most recent work is the two-volume *Black Women in America: An Historical Encyclopedia* (1993).

22419

973
NAR

Nardo, Don.

Braving the New
World, 1619-1784 :
from the arrival of
the enslaved
Africans to